THE REAL WORLD OF FAIRIES

THE REAL WORLD OF FAIRIES

A First-Person Account

DORA VAN GELDER

A publication supported by
THE KERN FOUNDATION

Quest Books
Theosophical Publishing House

Wheaton, Illinois ◆ Chennai (Madras), India

Second Edition 1999
Fifth Printing 2018

Quest Books
Theosophical Publishing House
P. O. Box 270
Wheaton, IL 60187-0270

www.questbooks.com

Library of Congress Cataloging-in-Publication Data

Kunz, Dora.
  The real world of fairies: a first-person account /
by Dora van Gelder.—2nd. ed.
    p.   cm.
ISBN 978-0-8356-0779-7
1. Fairies. I. Title.
BF1552.K86   1999
133.9—dc21   99-12297
                                              CIP

Printed in the United States of America

10 9 8 7 6 * 18 19 20 21 22

❧ CONTENTS ❧

❧ FOREWORD ❧

by CAITLÍN MATTHEWS

It is my pleasure to introduce the reader to the visionary encounters of Dora van Gelder in this new edition of *The Real World of Fairies*. The openhearted experiences of the writer reveal a wondrous realm which many will recognize from their own childhood, wherein each tree was inhabited by its native spirit and certain mysterious places held the possibility of joyful communion with our companions and neighbors of the natural world: beings unseen to most adults.

It is my place in this foreword to help set the author's writing within the context of our contemporary understanding of the fairy realms. Within Dora van Gelder's lifetime—a span that includes most of the twentieth century—fairies have undergone an interesting transition in popular consciousness.

In 1907–10, when W. Y. Evans-Wentz of Stanford University visited Britain, Scotland, Ireland, Wales, and Brittany for his outstanding study, *The Fairy Faith in Celtic Countries*, he learned that belief in and encounters with fairies was a living tradition still.[1] These fairy traditions are still a daily part of people's everyday experience in Celtic countries. They are the latter end of a long fairy tradition stretching back beyond the Middle Ages into the Celtic past. First-person documentation of this tradition is sporadic but consistent. Here are two instances of fairy encounters which involve clergymen—one Catholic, one Protestant—to demonstrate that seeing fairies has little to do with one's spiritual orientation!

A thirteenth-century account by the chronicler Gerald of Wales tells of Elidyr, a Welsh boy who went into the fairy hills. He found the subterranean realm of the fairies, a sunless realm of great beauty. The fairies were keepers of their word and had only the greatest contempt for mortal ambitions and lies. Elidyr learned the fairy tongue, which was a little like Greek. Due to adult mortal greed, which sent him back into Fairy to seek for gold, he eventually lost the way back and was forever after unable to return, as Elidyr subsequently related with tears of sorrow.[2]

The fairy researches of the seventeenth-century writer Rev. Robert Kirk remain the earliest semi-anthropological study of fairy customs and mores. Kirk himself is believed not to be in his tomb in Aberfoyle but to be in the fairy realms to this day. Kirk interviewed people who had encountered the fairies and knew of their ways. Several facts which he noted about them appear throughout the Celtic tradition: that they have their own underground dwellings which mortals tend to avoid, that they are apt to steal human children and substitute changelings in their places, that they are keepers of treasures, that they can form helpful alliances with humans.[3]

Fairies appear in world traditions under many different names, of course, and remain a vigorous source of wonder, disquiet, or disbelief, depending on the degree of modernism in the country in question. But something has radically changed in this century. The process began when folklorists and story collectors, like the brothers Grimm, began to research stories in the early nineteenth century. Country people—significantly adults— told stories and songs of fairies as defensive warriors, beguiling lovers, keepers of treasures and wisdom. With an eye to a wider readership, story collectors began to change things. The more robust elements of fairy lore were purged until the term *fairy story* began to mean "a light folktale suitable for children."[4]

After the Age of Reason, wherein anything unseen was held not to exist, there was an upsurge of interest in the supernatural and the esoteric during the nineteenth century. Those researchers most interested in the field were disconnected from their own living fairy and magical traditions and looked to the mysterious East for their inspiration, neglecting the treasure that lay all about them.

R. J. Stewart, a leading authority on fairy traditions, states that between the living fairy folk traditions of the world and the view of fairies now part of contemporary culture there is a world of difference. The image of fairies as small winged beings attendant on flowers owes more to the idea of devas or nature spirits popularized by nineteenth-century productions of *A Midsummer Night's Dream* than to the view of fairies long held by our ancestors.[5]

At the end of the nineteenth century, interest in psychic phenomena took a more scientific and quantifying turn. New technology was brought to bear upon the capturing of ectoplasmic contacts, ghosts, and apparitions. The camera could not lie— or could it? The Cottingley fairy photographs taken by two little girls in 1917 caused a considerable stir in Theosophical circles. It was a hoax to which Sir Arthur Conan Doyle unwittingly lent his endorsement. In 1983, Elsie Wright, one of the little girls who took the photographs, then in her eighties, admitted to having faked the evidence from cardboard cutouts. The Cottingley fairy incident recently sparked two films, *Photographing Fairies* (1997) and *Fairy Tale* (1997), each of which dealt differently with the whole nature of the fairy phenomena.

Today there is a growing interest in fairy traditions as they may be applied to the pagan revival. This movement sometimes swerves between the whimsical and the fantastic, but it does have a historical root: country people in Britain who were arrested and accused of witchcraft in the sixteenth and seventeenth centuries spoke of meeting with the Fairy Queen rather than with the Devil. The novels of modern fantasy writers like Charles de Lint sustain and develop the traditional view of fairies as allies, challengers, and lovers, and have become very popular among pagans.

Several once strongly held traditional fairy beliefs have altered over the last twenty years. Crop circles—once believed to be the work of fairies—and abductions of humans into the fairy realms have now been put at the door of aliens, as popular belief shifts from a planetary to an interplanetary focus. Instead of having a proper regard for our terrestrial neighbors the fairies, to whom country people have been leaving offerings of milk and other gifts for centuries, our postmodern culture has reached the ultimate disconnection from the earth by seeking for extraterrestrial explanations.

The traditional view of fairies as spirits who must be addressed and treated with respect is now vested in extraterrestrials, who are cast as the baddies of the piece, while fairies are now viewed as akin to the angels, wholly good and useful to human beings. We need to be careful in our discernment of spirits. While we must be open to the possibility that we may indeed entertain angels unawares, we must also beware of being overly naive and accepting of every spirit we meet. Spirits, like people, come in all shapes and sizes. Some are well disposed towards us; some are indifferent to us; others will react strongly if we overstep the limits of good behavior.

Our view of the fairies has altered radically, but I wonder whether the fairies themselves have ever really changed?[6]

Dora van Gelder stands as an important commentator on fairy encounters for the twentieth century. As a clairvoyant aware of the world as a joyous and animated place, she experiences fairies as the elemental forms of nature, from the standpoint of a formative, pristine perception.

In approaching the experiences of Dora van Gelder, I am aware of how varied are the human accounts of fairy encounters. I have only my own to draw upon in a comparable way. My greatest wish as a child was to see a fairy. I used to lie in bed and pray with great earnestness to see one. Adults told me that fairies were to be found "at the bottom of the garden," and so, dutifully, I would go and stand among the nettles and thistles and look for fairies. But I was destined to be disappointed on each of these vigils because fairies do not show themselves to obsessive sightseers, such as I was then.

In fact, what I hadn't realized was, *I had already met and was friends with many fairies.* You see, I had been confused by the literature. My childhood books had pictures of fairies: small, humanoid beings of diminutive size with little gauzy wings like those of butterflies. In these books, fairies lodged in acorn cups and ate off mushroom tables. They were always depicted like country children, happy, rosy, and good-natured. *This* was what I expected to see.

My actual experience of fairies had been going on for some time, but I didn't know that was what they were. It took me many wasted years to recognize them. My favorite game as a child was to lie on the floor under a knitted woolen blanket of many colors that my mother had made for me. I would tuck in this blanket round my body and over my head so that I could meet with my friends, the Shapers.

The Shapers came to me in the semidarkness of the blanket. They came as shapes and colors, almost like the shapes that you see in a kaleidoscope. They turned and flowed in many different patterns. They came as smells, tastes, movements, and music as well. I loved them wholeheartedly, for they taught me and talked to me through their movements, patternings, and sounds. I say "talked," but they did not use speech, nor did I "hear" them with my ears. They communicated in shapings, reordering their primordial patterns in complex dances that taught me primal forms of knowledge.

As I remember this experience with my adult perceptions, the Shapers might resemble nothing more than the intricate tracery of nuclei viewed through a microscope. Yet despite their geometric and abstract appearance, the Shapers were the fairies that I sought for in vain.

It is no wonder that I did not associate them with the fairies in my picture books. Not only did they not resemble winged children, but the Shapers taught me deep earth-shattering knowledge concerning music and sound, about creation and the relationship of cause and effect, about metaphor and symbol. This experience was like being taught a language deeper than speech, one that transcended space and time.

I learned that the Shapers could be found in nature, in the woods that I explored every week alone—always safe with them to look after me. I knew they were in the chalk hills, the dew-ponds, the fallen trees that were my playmates, the fields of grain, and the secret, hidden, forgotten places of nature. The pathways shown to me by the Shapers in my childhood make sense to me now. I have come to understand the patterns, frequencies, and music of their teaching, as I use frequency, sound, and music in my practice to understand what ails people and as a healing agent for their soul hurts.

The spiritual gifts of the fairies are available only by prayer and by a willingness to be very courteous in return. My fairy allies frequently bring me into contact with the spirits of herbs, plants, and trees that help to heal hurts of body and soul. It is my custom every day to offer food to the fairies with a song of thanks, in order to maintain good neighborly relations.

Perhaps there are many people who, like me, always wanted to meet a fairy? Many of my students express a keen interest in finding fairy allies of their own. The fairies do not like to be noticed all the time; they need their own space and quietness, just as humans do. While they are often glad to help us, they are also secretive and retiring. Often we need to make changes in ourselves before they will make themselves known to us.

To find fairy allies we need to go with an honest heart, a lack of egocentricity, good manners, a sense of respect for others, and a keen, streetwise perception. Friendships come about through mutual attraction, likeness of spirit, and a willingness to reciprocate. Those who go with a consumerist spirit, with the aim of finding out what the fairies can do for them, will be sadly disappointed.

Dora van Gelder asks why more people do not see fairies. It seems evident that the majority of adults are too immersed in the physical side of reality to be aware of what is happening all around them in the unseen—and just as real—reality. Modern culture pays little heed to unseen reality and hence has little respect for cause and effect.

FOREWORD

I myself am not a "see-er" of phenomena, but rather someone whose hearing and touch combine to create perception of the resonant field. However, a few years back I had a brief experience of "the second sight" or *an dha shealladh*, as spiritual seership is called in Gaelic. Returning home from a grueling trip abroad, in a state of semistarvation, I began literally to see fairies with my physical eyes. The fairy folk who lived in the trees, plants, and streams leapt out at me from every direction. They didn't look like the Shapers at all. They looked like powerful, tall spirits, not many of them rosy and jolly, and certainly none of them with little wings! It was a very disturbing experience. In Estonia, I had been very much aware of the presence of fairies in the undisturbed enclave of the national forest. At home, in Oxford, I was actually *seeing* fairies at last, just as I had wished.

Plucking up courage, I began to ask them, "How is it I can see you in this way?" They replied, "You don't normally see us because of the hard stone [concrete roads] and the harsh light [electric street lights]. But we abide in the wild places still." As I spoke to them, I began to realize that this state of consciousness was a very dangerous one to remain in. I could very easily slip away into the fairy realms. I returned home and ate three meals, one after the other. Then I went to sleep. On awakening, I had the second sight no more, to my great relief!

Many traditional and ancestral teachings about the fairy folk recommend caution: people who are vulnerable should not seek out the fairies or visit their haunts. I can quite understand how babies, children, the lovelorn, and stray domestic animals can be drawn into the realms of Fairy never to return. The realms of the otherworld are indeed beautiful, but fairy ways are not human ways, and we shouldn't confuse the two.

In Ireland it is still a great breach of courtesy to tamper with the traditional haunts of fairy folk, and most country people are very careful to avoid such places. It is still considered a terrible thing to take wood from, let alone cut down, a fairy thorn tree.

A recent case revealed this to me in a shocking way. My client Michael asked for soul healing for himself concerning the death of his younger sister some years before. As I began to journey in spirit towards my spirit allies, my way was suddenly blocked by a fairy man in a great rage. He told me that Michael's family had injured his family, that unless Michael was prepared to plant a thorn tree as reparation, I could not go any further and get help for him. My own allies urged me to accept this agreement on Michael's behalf. They further told me that the fairies had been taking the souls of children from Michael's family in recompense for a terrible insult.

When I told Michael about the fairy man's anger and his demand for a thorn tree to be planted, Michael's face grew white. He stopped me suddenly and told me about his grandfather, who had unaccountably cut down an ancient fairy thorn tree. Michael told me that in every branch of his family since that day a young child had died. Michael promised solemnly that he would not only plant a thorn tree on his land and dedicate it to the fairies in recompense, he would also ensure that no one ever touched the tree, not even prune it! It is a promise I am sure he will keep.

Such stories demonstrate the relationship between cause and effect. No one may act with intention and expect to avoid the consequences. Because our popular consciousness of fairies has changed, because we give little heed to the unseen reality, and because we have so little respect for the earth itself, we need to exercise care about our behavior. As Dora van Gelder points out, the impact of pollution upon the environment has made the world a colder, harder, more lifeless place.

As she states, those who work closely with the elements have a keener respect for the delicate relationship between realities than most other adults. She cites sailors and miners as people who have a natural respect for the spirits of nature. Fewer people now work directly with nature. Sealed off in offices, exiled from earth on the fourteenth floor, many have no sense of the seasons' turning, of their own belonging to the cycles of nature. This lack of contact robs us of vitality, nurture, and spiritual health. Innumerable minor ailments and discontentments testify to our neglect of essential contact with nature. Yet it is to the healing power of nature that many now look.

Today, with rising concerns about health and environment, more people are turning to herbal remedies and plant extracts. Those who have contacted the spirits of flowers and trees in the quest for healing have discovered the harmonious corrective secreted in healing plants. When we take such medicine for ourselves, we align ourselves with the spirit of Fairy; with such remedies, we hold the key to the world's cure in more than one sense.

More and more people are now coming to a rather shocking awakening: that the earth and its resources are not commodities but the habitat of our species. We have shared this environment for ages uncounted with our fairy neighbors, but have been late to realize that it is the fairies and spirits of nature who have been preserving our planet, while we have been eroding its joys by our thoughtless behavior.

The further we grow from our earthly origins, the more we tinker with the sacred web of life, the more synthetic foodstuffs and medicines we take into our bodies, the further we grow from our fairy neighbors.

As Dora van Gelder points out, children sense the fun and the cooperative aspects of fairies. Bumbling adults very often act "off-beam" from their authentic selves and so can have less happy encounters. Our species has shown such great disrespect to the earth and its hidden inhabitants that we shouldn't automatically expect such simple, uncomplicated encounters as those experienced by the author.

The alliances and friendships we can have with the fairy world must begin with an awareness that we are all children of the earth and that respect is owed to all living beings. As we see from our experience in world politics, wherever there is a touchpoint of conflict, there also are peacemakers. This is our task: to be good ambassadors of our own species, to be willing to make the changes within ourselves rather than at the expense of other beings. The more people realize this, the better the chances for peaceful cohabitation.

Wherever we go about the earth, we must acknowledge the fairies and spirits of the land. It is especially important when we are preparing the ground to build a house or plant a garden. We can sit quietly in that place and listen carefully to the fairies. Tune into the quality of the place. Cease to worry about your own concerns. Become one with the land, the grass, the trees, the birds. Feel the land as if you were a part of it. Remember that you are indeed a child of the universe, just as much as the animals, flowers, hills, and rocks.

Perhaps, if you sit for long enough with the right kind of listening, you will become aware of the fairies of that place. Then you will be privileged to learn that the fairy folk are special guardians of the wild and deep places of nature.

Human beings have an arrogance that is abhorrent to fairies. It is only when we can lay aside our pride, our idea of ourselves as the summit of creation, that we can see and work with the fairies. This is not achieved by reading a book or attending a weekend course. This is a long, organic learning that spans years. But, if we are patient and courteous, we too can find fairy allies in the wild places of nature, in the secret pathways of our dreams, in the deep wisdom of the ancient and ancestral traditions of our land, as Dora van Gelder has demonstrated.

> This prayer is for all who are seeking a way to contact the fairy folk:

> In the veils between the worlds, I remember the fairy folk who guard the ancient places. May we walk lightly and with courtesy upon the earth, may no being stay their progress or block their path, so that the hidden household of the earth may be peaceful.[7]

It is Dora van Gelder's greatest wish that the divisions between ourselves and fairies may lessen and that a true cooperation may grow. The outcome of the future lies in all our hearts.

1. W. J. Evans-Wentz, *The Fairy Faith in Celtic Countries* (London: Oxford University Press, 1911).

2. Gerald of Wales, *The Journey through Wales* (Harmondsworth: Penguin, 1977).

3. Robert Kirk, *The Secret Commonwealth*, ed. Stewart Sanderson (Cambridge: D. S. Brewer, 1976).

CAITLÍN MATTHEWS

4. Caitlín Matthews and John Matthews, *The Fairy-Tale Reader* (London: Thorsons, 1993).

5. R. J. Stewart, *The Living World of Fairy* (Glastonbury: Gothic Image, 1995).

6. Peter Narvaez, ed., *The Good People* (Lexington: University Press of Kentucky, 1991).

7. Caitlín Matthews, *Celtic Devotional* (New York: Crown, 1996).

Caitlín Matthews is the author of thirty-one books, including *Singing the Soul Back Home: Shamanism in Daily Life*, *The Celtic Tradition*, and *The Celtic Spirit: Daily Meditations for the Turning Year*. Caitlín has a shamanic practice in Oxford which has helped many clients in search of healing, reintegration of soul, and vocational direction. With her husband, writer John Matthews, she teaches courses on shamanism and Celtic traditions worldwide.

1

INTRODUCTION TO
FAIRY WORLDS

Many people are willing and even longing to believe in the existence of fairies. The Little People are so bound up with happy memories of childhood that they are recalled with delight as part of a less materialistic world. But, to most of us, they stand as a lost illusion. Not so with everyone, fortunately. For I, amongst others, have seen all kinds of fairies for as long as I can remember, and I still see them daily. By *seeing* I mean that they are as much outside me as trees and are seen just as objectively.

In the following pages I propose to make these delightful beings as much a reality for you as I can. It is best that I try at the outset to make it clear why I have some special advantages for this enterprise. For one thing, having been born in the East, I have never been discouraged in my observations of fairies, because there are many people there who do see—and very many more who believe in—fairies. For this and other reasons, the not uncommon power among children to see them has in me persisted. Then, I have had the good fortune to fall in this life among family and friends who included several who could also see; and travel has enlarged the list. Therefore, what I have here set down is not the imagination of an isolated child. It is information gathered from many contacts and conversations with fairies all over the world in circumstances perfectly natural, however unusual. One can communicate with these beings in just as definite a manner as we human beings talk to one another—more so, for though the method (which I shall describe shortly) is slightly different, it is more rapid than speech, and, in some ways at least, it is a more accurate exchange.

It is important to mention these things, for once we see the world from the fairy point of view, we get a glimpse of a new universe. So many things that matter very much to us do not seem to matter at all to them. Life and death, for instance, are things that they know all about; to them there is no uncertainty and no tragedy involved. Human beings so often shrink from life and fear death. Fairies actually see the flow of life through all things. We live in a world of form without under-standing the life force beneath the forms. To us the loss of the form means the end of the life, but fairies are never deceived in this way. They have a penetrating and powerful lesson for us.

Why do most people not see fairies? They live in the same world as we do, but their bodies are less dense than ours, though only slightly less dense than a tenuous gas. I feel sure that the veil between them and us is exceedingly thin—so thin that nearly anyone could penetrate it with a little effort along the right line. The difficulty is to indicate this line and especially to get others to comprehend it. Most certainly, one strong reason for our not seeing them is due to a difference in point of view. If, therefore, what I write here can help to change points of view toward the fairy world, it will help to make more and more people able to see them.

That, of course, is not all. A special sense must be awakened in people if they are to see fairies. The kind of world fairies live in does not affect our ordinary senses directly. They cannot be touched or felt, yet they can certainly be seen. In fact, ordinary sight is a help in seeing them, but that sense by itself is a little too coarse to catch the light they give off. However, everyone has latent in them a sense finer than sight, and a number of people—a surprisingly large number—have activated it. It is this higher sense perception which is employed in watching the antics of the fairy world. After all, everyone has a wide range of sensory equipment. Touch reveals solids, taste tells us about liquids, and the sense of smell reports on gases. Sight is still more subtle, and the series does not end there. There is a force of special seeing called *clairvoyance*—clear seeing.

The fact is that there is a real physical basis for clairvoyance, and the faculty is not especially mysterious. The power centers in that tiny organ in the brain called the *pituitary gland*. The kind of vibrations involved are so subtle that no physical opening in the skin is needed to convey them to the pituitary body, but there is a special spot of sensitiveness just between the eyes above the root of the nose which acts as the external opening for the gland within. It feels as if one were looking from that spot on the forehead, just as it feels in ordinary sight as if one were looking with one's eyes, although we all know we are only looking through them. Perception through that sensitive spot differs from perception through the conventional sense organs in one way: within there is no nervous structure of the ordinary physical sort. But the perception works just as I have said, nevertheless. When it is necessary to look into that finer world in which the fairies and similar kinds of living beings exist, it is only necessary to concentrate for a moment along that line of sight, and the sense responds much as if the eyes (but in this case a single eye) has opened. I am told (for I do not pretend to be very well informed about biology) that there was once, in primitive animals ancestral to humans, a connection for the pituitary body to the skin and an outer opening for it. The present pituitary body is supposed to be an atrophied remnant from those days. But doctors know that the gland is far from being a useless remnant, for it secretes from both parts of itself some of those bodies which are an invisible part of the blood stream and have such a powerful influence on growth and other functions. So the pituitary gland is certainly very much alive and important in human beings. And it certainly has this use for receiving very fine vibrations from a world of things which are subtler than anything we know. I wish I could make it still clearer, but perhaps that is the best one can do. Maybe in a way it is just as well that this sense is not so readily at hand that people could force it to work. For any such violent effort to move nature ahead of her own time is in many cases fraught with danger. People sometimes try to press themselves forward into a clairvoyant state by using their will, taking drugs, or engaging in other practices. However, if its development is unnatural, clairvoyance is not usually safe. But this does not make it less real than in cases where the power occurs in a perfectly normal way.

The question will be asked why more people cannot see fairies. I suppose part of the answer is that almost nobody tries after they are grown up, or even in childhood for that matter, and the rest of the answer is that the few who know that fairies exist do not always try to see them in the right way. Toward the end of these pages I will have something to say about this, and so the matter may stand for the present. As far as I am concerned I can see fairies. I can see them with my eyes shut, but I do not close my eyes ordinarily, as it is for one thing unnecessary, and for another, when clairvoyant sight has brought fairies into range, ordinary sight helps very much to observe details. And many fairies are so nearly perceptible by ordinary sight that it is much easier to study them with that. Just what sort of light they give off or reflect (for they are themselves luminous) I do not know, for I am not a physicist, and even if I were, where are the instruments with which to study anything so subtle? A scientific friend suggested looking at fairies with and without some borrowed spectacles, by way of making some sort of test about the kind of light that is involved. I did so and found that the fairies looked different through the spectacles, just as trees look different. But perhaps the distortion is due to the effect upon one's ordinary sight. Again, fairies seem not so visible through ordinary window glass, but the same difficulty arises here as before: is it the dimming of light to ordinary eyes that is affected? Experiments of this sort need the help of a number of people who can see and, to be of any use, would have to extend over a long period of time. It is best just to set down such facts as seem important and go on to the whole question of what fairies are like, for that is the main purpose we have in view.

I should first say that in that invisible world there are many different kinds of creatures and activities besides fairies. It is not the purpose of this book to dwell on these others, yet some of them are so closely connected with the life and work of fairies that I shall have to mention them in their proper places.

Therefore, I must explain that there are two important forms of life which are related to fairies and are a part of that kingdom of nature. In fact, fairies are part of a great evolutionary line that parallels the human. It starts, as the human line does, with some exceedingly primitive forms and rises up through the fairies (who are themselves at various stages of evolution) and has as its highest beings those that are traditionally called "angels" or "devas." The fairies stand more or less in the same relation to angels as animals stand to humans. Almost all fairies are concerned with the processes of nature, as I shall describe later, and many of the angels are also. Angels are not the theme of this book and are discussed only as they are connected with fairies, but I would like to say in general that conventional ideas about them are on the whole pretty far from the fact. Angels are more interesting in themselves, as they really exist and live, than the ordinary beliefs allow them to be. Something of this will appear as we go on. The conventional idea of angels has never appealed to me, for it portrays them as beings with all sorts of virtues but very little character, whereas in reality angels have vivid individualities and are most fascinating. They are strong beings, not at all negative or weak. One factor in the popular belief about angels is correct, and that is that they are superior in intelligence to humans. A great many are very far superior, of course—magnificent beings. Similarly, many fairies are far more intelligent and highly developed than animals. I think fairies as a whole are more evolved than animals as a whole. This too will appear as we go on, as we give specific cases and examples.

The lower beings in this evolutionary stream may be called "elementals," because their life is little organized, and they, much like the elements, have almost no feeling and, of course, no thought. They are usually small but vary greatly in size and are enormously varied in character and function. But we need not concern ourselves very much with them, except where they occur naturally in the accounts of fairies. Elemental life, like that of fairies, is also in close touch with human beings. Fairy life, which is quite distinct from elemental forms although it proceeds from them in an evolutionary sense, has many remarkable contacts with the human line. It is not quite so easy to get into contact with angels, however. The matter of which an angel's body is made is very much finer than that of fairy bodies, and it is not visible at all to the physical eye. Angels require a pure form of clairvoyance for observation, so fine is the material of which their bodies are made. Thus, while angels are almost never seen with the physical eye, fairies can be seen in that way, especially out of the corner of the eye. A number of people can see fairies on the fringe of vision. The theory is that the central part of the retina is used so much for ordinary sight that it does not respond to the more delicate vibrations of light from fairies, whereas the rest of the retina is fresh and more suitable for such uses. Something of the relationship of the elemental life with the highest form of all, the angels which crown that evolutionary line, will be found in a later chapter.

I must make it plain that I have, in this book, described only a few of the thousands of kinds of fairies that exist. I want no one to suppose that I think I have seen all the kinds there are. Whether they are as numerous and varied as insects, birds, mammals, and fish I cannot say, but they do exist in great variety and abundance. I suppose that different and accurate names will, in due course, be given to all the sorts and kinds. In fact, in different mythologies names are given. But I have avoided these old terms. They have so many associations with mere belief, not with knowledge, that they are a distraction from the discussion of fairies as actualities. Furthermore, a number of preconceived ideas spring into people's minds when such terms as *elf, troll, undine,* and the like are used. These ideas are sometimes right and sometimes wrong, so (to be safe) I have ignored most of these old terms and coined such descriptive names as seemed to me more useful. Also, I have called the whole kingdom "the fairies." Sometimes these beings are generally classified as nature spirits, the term *fairy* being reserved for one special type belonging to the woods or garden. This, perhaps, is a good idea for the sake of accuracy, but the term *fairy* is so much more generally understood that I have used it for the whole kingdom.

There is one division within the kingdom which is quite as clear as divisions found in the world of animals and plants, and that is between fairies of the various elements. Therefore, I have arranged the descriptive part of this book to conform to the great natural divisions of fairies, namely, those of water, fire, air, and earth.

For the fairies of water are quite distinct from those of any other element; air supplies varieties which are different from the rest just as birds are different from fish or insects. This gives a natural and inevitable classification and one in which less departure from physical experience is involved. The groups merge into one another, just as in our solid world, some fish can fly a bit, and some land creatures can swim. But it is nevertheless a clear-cut and real division.

However, there is among them all, one type that most completely characterizes the term *fairy*. This is the common woods or garden fairy who figures frequently in these pages. He is to be found everywhere, and he varies as much from continent to continent as nationalities vary among human beings. Perhaps the best way to plunge into our subject is to take one of these land fairies and describe him at some length, in the hope that with his aid and in his companionship, we can enter freely and happily in the kingdom of these very real and truly delightful and friendly folk.

2

DIALOGUES WITH LITTLE PEOPLE

Our world already touches the fairy world at some points. Many people feel more or less truly the spirit of a wood or the grandeur of a mountain, but they attribute it too often to extraneous sights and sounds and sensations, whereas it often arises largely from the fairy world within. Poets like A. E., James Stevens, Yeats, Tennyson, and Shakespeare have enriched our knowledge of and feeling for the fairy world. They have known and known truly. A much larger number of people than is commonly supposed are in close communion with fairies and angels. The gap between the two groups of beings, fairies and humans, is not nearly so wide as our ignorance assumes. If we could only realize that we live in a world crowded with fairies, angels, and all manner of beings, it would make an immense difference in our attitude and our mode of living. The mere belief that such a world exists should delight us, the knowledge and certainty would follow in due course. We ourselves would become much more alive, for it is impossible to get into touch with that world, which thrills with the sense of being alive, without ourselves catching the same spirit and our own creative energy being awakened.

I was only one of many children who have known of fairies from the very earliest years, but in my case—owing to my good fortune and perhaps special advantages—this knowledge has not only persisted but widened. The reader may know of cases like this; I also have met many children who see and many more adults who still remember the days when they had this power. But not many have the courage to own up to their faculties, for often they are afraid of being thought peculiar. The very way so many parents treat children puts them on the defensive in the matter. Being spanked for "telling lies" is no encouragement to pursue the subject further. It makes the child ashamed of a lovely experience. Furthermore, we must remember that the whole business of seeing fairies is a delicate operation at best. The power to see requires conditions of quiet and peace; and then, fairies are themselves quite as shy as wild creatures and have to be tamed and attracted. Altogether, even under the best circumstances, especially around cities, the undertaking is not easy for the inexperienced. Add to this the ignorant hostility of the majority and, what is more, a fixed belief that only the dense material is real, and one can begin to appreciate the problem faced by the seeing child. Fortunately, more and more parents are becoming aware of nurturing creative abilities and higher sense perceptions in their children.

People who live close to nature, such as peasants and farmers the world over, know of fairies. The evidence is as incontrovertible in its mass and source as it is important in its nature and consequences. It is important, therefore, to set down instances of contact between the two kingdoms.

The relation we could all have with fairies can be illustrated by one incident. Many years ago some friends celebrated my fourteenth birthday with a picnic at National Park in Australia. In the party there were others who could see, and as we sat on the bank of the main stream in the park, we remarked on the numbers of curious and friendly fairies peering at us from the bush. This was our first visit to the park, and the wealth of fairy life led us to get in touch with the angel of the area. He proved to be a remarkable character, of great stature, and with an air of power and determination. He was accustomed to rule and carry out his plans, but in a way imbued with great kindness. He had been attracted to one member of our party who wore a jeweled cross, everywhere a symbol of power, and in this case a jewel with a very special radiation of light. So the angel remarked on it and said as much to us. He was interested to find that we were capable of talking to him and seeing fairies. He wanted to know all about the cross and even expressed a desire to have something of a similar nature, and asked us if we could not get him one. We were, of course, curious to know what made him want such a thing, and he explained. It appeared that he was ensouling this great valley and that he had a scheme for it. He had divided the valley into three parts, and in each place he wanted a different influence to be maintained. To this end he placed in and along the lower basin, which was tidal, a certain kind of fairy which is to be found in the sea, and also an intermediate sort which inhabits brackish waters, and higher, on the land, some gnomes and some emerald green fairies. Then, above this, there was a weir and quiet water, and in and around this he had established particularly fine sweet water fairies, a light powder or turquoise blue in color, very human looking, and on the surrounding land many sky blue woods fairies and many splendid little butterfly fellows.

Still higher up the stream, where it grew inaccessible and wild, he kept up a third atmosphere, with fairies of a kind more aloof from humanity. He wanted a jewel cross put somewhere in the central section of the valley to establish a center or point of influence for that part of the area. We were interested in all this and promised to get him a cross if possible. He was exceedingly pleased with the idea and most grateful.

Our party sang songs, as one does on such occasions, and this brought fairies from all over the place, the angel looking on all the time. They crowded round and were amazed to find people who could talk to them and who appreciated what they were about. When it came time to go, they begged us to come back again.

In due course, a friend and I returned on the day we had appointed to give the angel the cross, but without it. As soon as we came down to the place, in fact, before we really got there, the angel's first question was, "Have you got the cross?" I explained that we hadn't, because it was not yet ready. At this he was extremely disappointed and said one really should keep one's promises, once given, and that such things do not happen in the angelic kingdom. That slips occur in our material world did not count with him. But we stayed and had an enjoyable time making friends with several pleasant fairies who were delighted to talk to us. For the angel's plan included helping human beings, who came there in thousands on holidays. He wanted to give them some vision of beauty and some feeling of rest, and the fairies were told to be as kind as possible to visitors and to try to understand them. So they were always curious about human doings and had more than the usual interest in finding a couple of human beings willing to talk to them and able to explain the vagaries of human behavior. Some points were mysterious to them. For example, holiday crowds played football there. The fairies could understand the running but did not make out why the ball was an object of such fierce pursuit. We never managed to make this clear, except to convey that it was a game. We promised the angel that we would come back and bring the cross without fail.

The cross was finally ready, and we took it down to the park. The angel explained to us where he wanted it put, but after walking a couple of miles and finding the place, we discovered it was particularly horrible, with a gruesomely unpleasant atmosphere due, I am bound to admit, to human misdeeds. We appealed to the angel, and he said that he wanted the cross in this unpleasant place just because it was so unsavory. He hoped the radiation of the jewel would set it right. We begged him not to insist on that but to select a lovely spot where it would do its work with help from the surroundings. He called another angel into the discussion, and finally it was decided to put the cross in a spot of great beauty and more centrally located. Accordingly it was concealed there, and the angel called at once all the fairies of the valley to the place. Thousands came to join the hundreds who already had been watching the business with great curiosity. The angel explained the purpose of the jewels, and he held then and there a ceremony to celebrate the acquisition. The fairies passed around in a circle in a slow winding dance, delightful in this addition to the beauties of the park. They were told by the angel to go there constantly and bathe in the radiation of the jewels and so carry the new influence about the park.

Such an episode is, of course, rare, but fairies in gardens every day are in touch with human beings. Generally when people come into a garden they know nothing about the fairies there. The fairies know the humans are there, but as there is no human response, they go about their own business.

They always take notice of children and especially of quite small ones, as they have much affection for children, who are in the human order the nearest things to them. If, however, we walk in a garden without seeing the fairies but imagine their presence, we are sure to get in touch with them, especially when we stop to admire the flowers. Sincere admiration of the flowers and the plants is a great source of gratification to fairies. If they see a human being who truly feels attraction for a special plant or flower, they take an interest in the admirer, as their vanity is flattered. They immediately think that person must be especially nice, and in this way a point of contact is established, for growing things is a common interest. Love for flowers and a conscious invitation to the fairies to help is a way to come to know them and perhaps even to see them. It is love of living things which is the great bridge between the two kingdoms.

The method of getting in touch with water babies (as I call them) is rather different. They are not at all shy or timid of human beings and so are willing to come near and make friends. They can help us considerably because of their overabundance of vitality, as will be discussed later. When I lived near the sea, we had a delightful way of getting into touch with the creatures of the water. Whenever we crossed the water on the ferry, I used to think of the sea fairies and invite them to come close to us. This they willingly did, as they thought it a lark. We used to amuse ourselves by looking around the boat until we found someone who looked miserable. Then we would ask one of the water babies if he would not go to that person and give him some of the sense of radiant happiness that is necessary to them. He would love to do this, so he would run up to such a person and try to shoot happiness into him, and very often we would see a change in the face and even the appearance of a smile. The fairy sometimes would stay about that individual for an hour or so trying to make him feel better. (These sea fairies can follow a person onto the land for a couple of hours but not very much longer.) This is something many people could try for themselves. The water baby likes to help, and to him it is all adventure. Some people feel, after such ministrations, as if they had had a refreshing meal, so substantial is the effect to a sensitive person.

The help does not always come from fairy to human being; neither is the contact between the two kingdoms always of a pleasant character.

A case illustrating this happened to me. One evening in Australia a few of us went for a walk along the point of land in Sydney harbor where a dear Little Fellow is to be found. As we approached this place, the first thing that was strange was the sensation of physical heat at a certain spot along the path, although it was a cool night and it had not been a warm day. At the same time, there was also a most unpleasant creepy feeling. We had until then no special thought of my little fairy friend, but at that moment we caught sight of him running as hard as he could away from this unpleasant spot. Just then he also saw us and turned and rushed towards us, delighted and relieved to see us. He told us that he was terrified, as some most unpleasant creatures of which he was really frightened had invaded his place. We found indeed that there were four or five big mon-ster-like creatures of a horrible color and feeling. They were playing in their own way and writhing about the spot. They were of a hideous red color, with monstrous caricatures of bison heads and shapeless bodies. They were the embodiment of some thoroughly unpleasant feelings resulting from some episodes involving humans which had taken place at that particular place. Something had gradually built up enough of an unpleasant emo-tional charge there so that, on this particular night, the negative feelings took this independent ele-mental shape. Our fairy friend begged for our help.

We tried to drive the beasts away, for they were of low intelligence, and none could be of any practical use. But they were obstinate, and no effort of will had much direct effect on them. But by chance we found they had a mortal fear of the sea, just close by, and by an effort of our more determined will, we finally dislodged them from the land, and they tumbled into the harbor and almost immediately melted from sight.

The Little Fellow never forgot this help and remained steadily our friend as long as we lived there. It is, however, more common to find fairies helping humanity than the other way around, for after all they are aware of us and are almost uniformly kindly, whereas we seldom know about them, and besides we are rather subject to moods—although moods do not last long in their presence! There is, in fact, a remarkable arrangement by means of which that world helps the people in this world of ours.

There is a whole department, as it were, composed of highly developed sylphs and often even angels who take part in the work. Many people have what is commonly called a "guardian angel." This is usually a sylph who is linked with a person at birth or baptism or through some other ceremonial occasion. Guardian angels are supposed to help their human friends, especially at critical times, taking special interest during the years of childhood, though very often the connection languishes later on. If, however, human beings were aware of the relationship, they could do much more to profit by it, for one's sylph is delighted to take part in the life of a person who responds to the sorts of things in which the sylph is interested. If the human partner is egocentric and is interested only in the more material sides of life, the sylph soon loses interest, although even then the sylph will help on occasion and during crises. But if the child shows increasing interest in things worthwhile and is being of use to others and generally outwardly turned and socially minded, then the presence and active aid of the sylph can continue for years. Sometimes the relationship is very beautiful. As a rule the sylph or the angel (in cases where it is an angel) is definitely more developed than the man or woman of the partnership and has the immense advantages of the fairy life, that is, its mobility, its cooperative spirit, and its beneficent outlook. For instance, the guardian may perceive that the child of its human friend is in some danger; the sylph then flashes into the feelings of the baby's mother the idea of danger and moves her to run and see just in time. Innumerable little things—and often more important events which happen in early life—bring the relationship into active being.

In childhood the relationship between the two kingdoms is closer than at any other time of life. This is because children are closer by nature to fairies than any other human beings. They are naturally happy and spontaneous in action; they fit well into nature; they are also somewhat irresponsible, with few worries about food and clothing; and they have a remarkable capacity for finding delight, fascination, and creative joy in little things like a pebble or a shell or an empty box. They also take an intense interest in young and growing things, are boundlessly curious about everything within range, have no consciousness of conventional traditions of behavior or moralities, and love adventure, dressing up, and tales of mystery and imagination. In all these ways children are close to the fairies in character. This is why in childhood the gates are so often open, and the human and fairy worlds are so completely one.

Among adults there are many individuals who are more or less aware of the fairy kingdom, but the only group of people who may be said to furnish a sort of test of the relationship are sailors. The physical conditions of their life naturally mark them; the hours they keep, with watches in the night, their life on the sea, secluded with the same small company for long periods at a time, the sense of detachment from ordinary human concerns— all these create a special environment. In those surroundings, however, the fairies also play a part. Sailors are the only group of human beings who are subjected almost exclusively for long periods at a time to the presence and atmosphere of two special groups of fairies: those of the sea and those of the air. Now the nature of these is quite different from the land types, as I have tried to make clear. Is it not likely that the traditional character of the sailor, his belief in the supernatural and in the power of the elements, is due to this special experience? Miners, it is true, are also subjected to a special kind of fairy world, but for one thing, theirs is part of the earth element, and for another, they return to the normal influences of the surface after a few hours. But the sailor becomes really saturated with the jovial yet strange power of the creatures of the deep sea and of the air.

I have frequently been in the company of people who can watch the fairies, but the number of such folk is necessarily small. I have personally known ten or twenty with this capacity and have studied the fairies together with them at various times. I am here referring only to people who see them whenever they desire. On occasion, I have also been with persons who have seen fairies for the first time. And at times I have gone to observe and describe fairies to persons at their request, when circumstances made it useful. For instance, I made a fairy hunt in Central Park in New York just to satisfy the demands of a metropolitan paper. I went there expecting to find none at all, but there were a few, even though it was quite early spring. In fact, they were rather interesting, as they seemed to have no fear of human beings since they saw them so constantly. If a person came near one, the fairy would retreat a little, but the fairy had no sense of being menaced. There were two kinds most in evidence. Some were of the small, twelve-inch emerald green kind. They were having a lovely time climbing about a hickory tree and were much too happy, jumping from branch to branch and rejoicing, because it was a good sunshiny day, to respond to me at all. I also saw a fairy in two shades of brown and gold, looking like a teddy bear with a chunky face, who was busily engaged with some bushes. I managed to get into conversation with him, and I tried to explain to him that he would be put into a newspaper and could he not say something special? He was intrigued with the idea of receiving attention, but could not grasp the idea at all. His notion of a newspaper was a thing people put in front of their faces and then threw about the park! Why they did this, and how he could be put into one of them and then be thrown on the ground, was quite beyond his capacity to take in. As for a special interview, after all he was there, the people were there, he liked them, and he particularly liked the children, and so what was it all about? He was an extremely matter-of-fact fairy, I am afraid. Nevertheless, even though the fairy life in the park provided nothing very particular, the fact that there were any fairies at all in the cities was of much interest at that time. I have, in the past, actually accompanied reporters on such fairy hunts—not that the reporters ever saw them. For there continues to be wide interest in the fairy world, even in our materialistic, science-oriented world.

Even though fairies have been supplanted in children's imaginations by more modern fancies, like creatures from outer space, they remain a deep, instinctive need of humanity. This yearning for their friendship and for the mere knowledge that they exist has its root in the fact that the fairies are there, silent and unseen to most people, yet close at hand—tapping, as it were, with elfin hands on the thin shell between the two worlds. The clear bell notes of their music can almost be heard. The gaiety and beauty which they embody presses in upon us from every bit of parkland, of wood, of garden. The sky and sea are joyous thresholds into their worlds. On every side there are fairies, and therefore on every side loveliness and happiness. If adults could but recapture the simplicity and directness of children even in some small degree, they too would recover the lost land of happiness that is the kingdom of the Little People, for the fairies would delight in becoming their simple friends, always to be depended upon, always kind.

3

A TYPICAL FAIRY

I t is not easy to give a detailed description of how fairies look or what their bodies are made of. First of all, there are the many different varieties. This problem can perhaps be best met by describing a more or less typical fairy, pointing out those characteristics that they all seem to share. The second obstacle lies in the fact that most of us find it difficult to conceive of bodies that are not made of physical matter. However, we understand from science that physical matter is itself nothing but energy patterns and waves; therefore, it should not be hard for us to think of the bodies of fairies as made of a kind of finer matter, more subtle than the rarest gas. In our world we need a more or less rigid body to resist stress and accident and pressure, and this results in all sorts of specialized structures such as the bony skeleton and the muscular and nervous systems. But the environment in which fairies live does not demand this rigidity. Gravity and density and pressure are altogether different, and a complicated and resistant form is not needed.

Since this is the universal state of affairs for fairies, what I am about to say of a selected individual fairy is more or less universally true.

For purposes of description, I shall take an ordinary fairy of the surface of the land, a common woods or garden fairy, which we may consider the most typical of them all. This kind may be said to be in midstream of fairy evolution; they are in constant touch with humankind, are found in various colors and sizes nearly everywhere on earth, and have been seen by many people. These fairies are, in fact, so common that it is easy to pick out an individual for analysis. This one happens to be a green fairy of the New England woods.

He is some two feet six inches tall, with a slender body and a head which is rather larger in proportion to his body than is common among adult human beings. His body is made of matter in a state much more like vapor than anything else we know of in our world, but the form is quite definite and lasting. The material of his body is as loosely knit as the vapor from the spout of a boiling teakettle and is somewhat of the nature of a cloud of colored gas. In fact it is exactly that, only the gas is finer than the lightest we know and is less readily detected even than helium or hydrogen. But this does not prevent it from being held together in a form, for it is not a chemical but a living substance which life saturates and holds together. In truth, his power over this matter as a living creature is shown by the fact that his body is composed of two distinct densities of material. The body proper is a true emerald green and fairly dense, considering the stuff of which it is made; around this on all sides, both front and back, is a much thinner cloud of the same matter in which he is not so vividly alive. This thinner portion, which extends from all sides of his body proper, is a lighter green.

All this material is virtually the stuff of which feelings are made. It is vital matter. The movements of our friend are due to his desire to be somewhere or to do something. Since the matter of which he is made is itself of the nature of living emotion, instead of involving a complicated system of veins, muscles and nerves when he feels an emotion, his body responds immediately and directly.

I must explain that although I see through the thinner outer part of his body, and although the denser part or body proper is so tenuous that one almost feels one sees into it, this does not prevent him from having some organic structure, although it is much simpler, I think, than any animal's physical body could be. The principal inner organ appears to be what we might call his heart, which is a glowing and pulsating center about where a human heart would be. This is golden light. It pulsates very much like a human heart but simply in and out. When he is active it is rapid, and when he is quiet it is slow. This organ is his center of vitality, and it appears to circulate vital currents all over him, so he has a primitive system of circulation that is a kind of blood and nervous system combined. The head has a special structure, but he is not much centered in his head, for his principal experience is through feeling and life. On rare occasions, when he is curious or tries to think, his head glows a little also with the same sort of golden light from within. As he never eats, he has nothing like a digestive system, but he has a mouth and other facial organs. Before I pass to the latter, however, I must mention that this heart center has one peculiarity. The fairy can control it, and that is how he gets into touch with things around him, particularly living beings. When he wants to respond to a plant, he makes his heart beat at the same pulse rate as the plant. This synchrony makes them unified. The secret of the fairy life is rhythm. Each kind of fairy (whether water, land, air, or fire) comes into the world with a limited and definite range of rhythmic power, according to his species and his own personal nature. Within this range, he controls the rhythm of vitality by his desires and feelings.

This heart rhythm is a matter of vital contact with things around him, but his sensations and responses to a stimulus from without works whether or not he is in synchrony of identity with the person or creature. That is, he has something corresponding to our sensory mechanism. He is all sensation, and so he does not get sense impressions exclusively through specific organs of perception like eye or ear, but rather in a general and yet vivid way all over him. He saturates himself in things that give him sensation. It is true, however, that this is rather more acute and specialized in certain parts of his body. For instance, he does have eyes of a kind, and he seems to turn in order to get a good look at a thing, but he can be well aware of something visible behind him because his whole body feels the radiation from it. His senses include a sense of smell—all over him—for he bathes in what is evidently the perfume of sweet-smelling flowers, but he also does the same thing with flowers which appear to me to have no fragrance at all. So he is more sensitive in this particular sense than we are, not less. He has no sense of taste, for being ephemeral, he does not eat, but he certainly receives sounds and responds to music, and here again, his response is all over his body. He has something like ear orifices and sometimes pointed ears, but I think the sound actually is received all over him, and the ears serve for interpretation in some way.

In the average fairy the facial features are rudimentary. The one sense that seems to be localized in a special organ is sight. For a fairy does not come and peer at one. The eyes are not well defined and, in most cases, have no lids or brows or lashes, for he has no need of such things. He often has a protuberance like a nose and, as a rule, suggestions of ears. His mouth is a line, within any wrinkles around it, and it curves a little to express feelings of amusement and pleasure (which his whole form in fact expresses far more vividly), but he rarely opens his mouth and does not appear to have any teeth. When he does grin, the mouth draws back and becomes longer in an amusing way, but no wrinkles form around it or around his eyes. His face is a soft tan and a sort of furry-looking mop of green mossiness surrounds it.

One singular fact is that when one looks at him sideways, his head is nearly as thick from front to back as his body, and he does not possess much of a neck. Another thing about these common woods fairies is that they either have long legs and a short body or short legs and a long body. They seldom exhibit the proportions familiar to us.

When our green friend moves, he does not walk from place to place, but floats. His desire draws him, or his need to be at some spot. Of course, when he wants to, he can hop about in lively fashion and jump up and down. He has legs and arms without much detail of fingers and toes, and a hand will often enough be like a foot. All the knotty muscles and sinews we see in the bodies of animals are lacking here. He is slender and graceful and quaintly agile.

So much for a detailed description of one of the myriad Little People. The rest must be extensive qualifications of all I have said. For there are many varieties, as I shall show, varying from minute creatures of an inch or two to huge monsters.

The individual fairy, even the particular little fellow I have just been describing, has the power of changing his shape and size in a remarkable manner. His body is feeling and vitality, and as he feels and lives, the shape and size alter. He can make himself quite small, say five or six inches, and he can swell up until he is five or six feet. But he would need to want very much to do this, and he could not remain this huge size indefinitely. Nor need he stay green. He can take on colors as well as shapes. In fact, one of the most delightful games among fairies is what I have always called "dressing up" in colors and clothes and coverings, according to their fancy.

Even in natural coloring the common woods and garden fairy varies greatly in different localities. Besides this sort with green body and tan face (found in numbers here in New England), I have seen horizontally banded scarlet and purple ones in Florida; in California, golden ones sometimes in solid color and sometimes striped with pale shades; in the northwestern states, blue and also delicate lavender; in northern California, bronze-hued, as if cast in a mold and often with singular marks like whorls over the body. On the French Riviera, there are lemon yellow and green fairies, again striped, and also some lovely blue and pink ones, with a few scarlet and yellow. In India, I remember particularly among the many kinds there a sort that is deep orange and another, scarlet. In Java, the most lovely and common sort is deep blue striped with gold. In Australia, the commonest sorts are sky blue, but I have seen some strange black and red fairies in the mountains there. Orange and yellow and orange and white striped kinds occur in certain of the South Sea Islands. This list will show that this type of land-surface fairy alone has immense variations in appearance. The natural color seems to have some sympathetic relation with the vegetation; in general, the appearance is brighter in tropical lands.

This same ordinary garden or woods fairy will serve for a detailed description of the place of fairies in nature's economy, but again it should be understood that I am describing only one of hundreds of kinds.

Perhaps the commonest of all sights in the world of fairies is their incessant activity among plants, shrubs, and other growing things. In every garden, on every strip of land where there is plant growth, one sees them busily engaged in constant care of living things. What exactly are they about, and how do their enterprises affect plants and animals? The answer is probably not simple, but I can at any rate describe exactly what I see.

I must first of all explain that a fairy does not see anything in the way we do. When we look at a rose bush we see only the form of stem, leaves, and flowers. But the fairy sees quite differently. From a few yards away the rose bud itself is to him a glowing object, rather larger than the physical rose we see. It appears to him not as something reflecting light but actually the source of phosphorescent-like light of its own creation. If the fairy comes nearer he perceives many details. At the point which we call the heart of the rose he sees a definite point of light, and from this radiate delicate lines of colored light which evidently correspond to the physical structure of the petals. There is a constant flow from the heart center along the lines of the blossom's anatomy. Now, there are two main currents involved. The plant itself draws food and moisture and strength from the earth, and all this passes up the stem in the digestive process and looks to the fairy like currents of light. Meantime the leaves and the blossoms are drinking in sunshine as well as carbon dioxide, and the sunshine supplies a second current. These two streams look like ascending and descending spirals of light in the stem of the bush, and so the rose bush also appears to the fairy as a structure of glowing colored light——fine lines which are brighter than the general brown and green and white structure of the bush. The rose heart is the distributing center of these energies for the blossom itself.

> The opening of a bud, the growth of a leaf, the astonishing development of beauty in a flower involve physical operations which completed chemical science would leave as far beyond our comprehension as

the difference between lead and iron, between water and carbonic acid, between gravitation and magnetism, are at present. A tree contains more mystery of creative power than the sun, from which all energy is borrowed. An earth without life, a sun, and countless stars, contains less wonder than the grain of mignonette.

[Kelvin, quoted in J. Arthur Thompson, *An Introduction to Science*, p. 150]

In this interchange of energies, those from the earth and those from the sun, the fairy plays a definite part. He has power over both these currents, especially the vitality from the sun. He can retard them here and accelerate them there, and he can add some extra vitality from himself at such points as he desires. He first of all puts himself into rapport with the plant by making his own heart center beat with the rhythm of the plant. He stands off and sizes up what he wants to do. Then he goes to work. He skips and hops all over the plant and pats it with touches of light which flow from his own hands into the streams of the plant. In this way he alters and adjusts its life. He likes to have a gay show of flowers, and so he is likely to keep an eye on this aspect, but his main duty is to make the plant do as well as possible under existing conditions. He might spend a busy ten or twenty minutes in this way.

After what he would consider a hard job done, he would probably leave the plant, make a somersault or two in the air, and then bound about and have a good time, just for the joy of being alive. Then he would resume his labors.

It may properly be asked, "Would plants grow without this aid?" They most certainly would, but the intervention of fairies (and the care given by human beings) makes the difference between scraggly and luxurious growth. Plants grow no doubt because of an inner urge to live and reproduce, as that is the dominant thing in all nature. But the help of fairies is just as important for the plant's full life as plowing is for the life of corn in a field. Why should we not take the fairy's own testimony? He himself feels that his work is a serious business, and in his own way, he takes his job as important. He feels responsible for everything the plant does and takes an almost maternal pride in its achievement. Besides, he has to show results to the fairy above him, who comes at intervals to see how things are progressing. It is astonishing how far this sort of work is carried. For instance, I have seen even in hot houses a kind of fairy at work over the tiny plants. This is a very much smaller sort of fairy, but the work they do is of the same order.

A great deal of the life of the fairy is spent in playing about, though where a line can be drawn between work and play is hard to say, for of course, looking after the plant he loves is fun to the fairy. He looks upon it less as a duty than as a pleasure which he should attend to faithfully. There are, in fact, only degrees of play in his life. And so, even in play, he is useful because of the happiness which he radiates and which often makes human beings and other creatures spontaneously happy when they come within its influence, even if they know nothing about fairies.

Play takes the form of jumping and skipping, peeping curiously into birds' nests, and taking an interest in all the show of life about. The fairies know all neighboring birds and animals personally and show deep concern in all their doings. The sense of mischief is well developed, and practical jokes are going on all the time. One fairy will steal into another's area and be found demurely doing the neighbor's rightful jobs, only to be hustled out gaily. They have a power of hypnotic suggestion over animals which can make a rabbit or a squirrel miss a bit of food which he starts out to get. These antics are just fun, and the animals are not irritated or really teased. Groups of fairies in forests can similarly put spells over human beings in small ways, but on the whole they leave us severely alone. They sit about at intervals and relate anecdotes to one another, and this takes an astonishing form. The fairy has an immense power of mimicry and a sense of drama. He is an emotional artist of rare ability, and a group of them will put on a show for mutual entertainment. I must explain again that a fairy has the power not only to change his form but also to clothe himself in marvelous garments, a process that is carried out by drawing the denser part of the material about him by means of his will power or desire into a thought garment. This requires effort and concentration and takes a few minutes to achieve, especially if he desires to change his form. The thought garment will last as long as he sustains the effort at transformation. Most fairies are deficient in concentration, and thus they do not keep up the show for any length of time. Because of this lack of sustained concentration and their lack of thoroughness in thinking out their disguise, whole parts of the makeup will be missing, or they may lack a limb or other important part. This often gives them a ridiculous appearance. When the failure is prodigiously exaggerated, even the fairies are uproariously amused, and the failure will himself skip about in glee—for any cause for fun is good. If, all of a sudden, for lack of concentration one of them slides right out of his part and is discovered in his normal role, it is enough often to suspend the whole performance. But when a show is well under way, they get into the spirit of the thing, and the show gambols along merrily. It is like the dream of a vaudeville show, without any sustained dramatic theme. It is all makeup and make-believe and go-as-you-please.

In Australia I once saw an amusing incident of this kind. In the moonlight there were four or five fairies playing about. They were telling one another stories and dressing up and acting out some bits of the tales. One fairy had dressed up in his idea of a king, which he got from some storybook indirectly through the thoughts of some child. And he was trying to look and feel very important and severe, with much flinging about of arms. Just as he was very intent upon being very royal and severe, he forgot his crown and his regal garments, and these fell from him with a devastating effect of revelation so complete that all the others rolled about with glee. This attempt reminded others of having seen a Masonic cornerstone-laying procession, and they tried to reproduce it, strutting about in such fragments of the regalia as they could recall and carrying out a mummery they did not in the least appreciate. I happened to know some of the people in the original Masonic affair, and the fairies' caricatures of them were faithful and very effective connotative cartooning.

Another source of fun is for the fairy to tell a circle of friends a tale that he makes up. The idea is to make it more and more improbable and wild. A sort of "contest in the imaginary" sets in, with perfectly hilarious results mixed with sudden moments of great gravity. I suppose this kind of life, which is, in the last analysis, all fun, would not meet with the approval of a serious and work-oriented humanity. But we must remember that fairies, like children, have an overabundance of vitality. They are not restrained by public opinion as we are. Indeed, their public opinion is in favor of it!

4

FAIRY LIFE

B etween the human point of view and that of a fairy, or any member of the angelic kingdom, one of the main differences is that we live in a world of *form*, and they live in a world of *life*. Our thoughts are primarily concerned with the form things have, and we seldom go further than that. But fairies are mainly concerned with the energy and life flowing around and within the form—life that is everywhere. For example, if we look at a tree we respond to its size, its shape, its color, its leaves, and fruit. These things combine to create its beauty for us. But when one comes to think of it, this is rather a limited way of seeing the world in which we live. In contrast, the fairy first beholds the spirit of the tree and responds to its vital energy. To a fairy, the tree is a living, breathing personality which is expressing itself in the form we see. There is then an exchange of feeling, a mutual response, between the fairy and the tree. Thus fairies live a life which is much less limited, much more interesting than ours. We humans are so hampered by the limitations of our senses that often we grow old too quickly out of sheer boredom with the dreadful monotony of our static world. We have feelings for the pets we are fond of, such as our cats and dogs, and a few exceptional human beings may feel something like a personal friendship with respect to trees or flowers. But the relationship between fairies and the creatures that live around them is so different as to be almost a new order of existence. Since this point is important, I should like to explain further.

Most of our world is composed of inanimate objects or things that appear to be dead. Not only are we ignorant of the true life of animals, plants, and rocks, but we are surrounded and our lives filled with *things*—just *things*—like chairs, tables, food, typewriters, cars, and television sets. Ours is a world of *objects*. But a fairy never experiences anything of this character. She lives in a world where every blade of grass and every leaf are thrilling with a sense of being alive. In her world nearly everything expresses itself in some form of rhythm. Grass has a certain kind of pulsing life, each tree is an individual friend, and the flowers, birds, insects, and fish are, to a fairy, like her children. Furthermore, she lives in a world of friendliness, with thousands of creatures that have no physical form. Everything, from the butterflies to the leaves floating in the wind, is filled with a riotous, joyous life, and she senses this and feels akin to them in just being alive. Her world pulsates with life, motion, feeling; these are its most essential characteristics.

Even one good look at the world in which the fairy lives is enough to convey this unique quality. It is not a world of surfaces—of skins and husks and barks, with definite separate edges and identities—but a state in which everything merges into everything else in an astonishing manner: Nothing is static; all is dynamic. Let us begin with the fairy herself. As one looks at her, one sees she has no skin. She is more or less a cloudy form. If you tried to touch her, there would be no point at which you could say, "This is her outer layer," because although she is increasingly dense as you penetrate toward her center, it is a gradual increase; there is no boundary of skin or fur to mark her off. In the same way, the trees and grass and everything else in her world are to her like a pillar of light or a spot of glowing color, melting and mixing and fading into the surroundings. It is like living in a fluid world in which creatures have shapes that are sufficiently definite to be perceived, but which are always glowing, transparent, changing, and mingling.

Because she lives in a world which throbs with life, the fairy looks at things in a way which is all her own. It is much simpler than ours. Fairies are realists, far more than we are. They have no complex and complicated emotions and ideas such as we have, because they have no sense of possession and no fear or envy. Therefore they have no illusions, but rather have the power of seeing clearly and coming straight to the point. It is true that they play at dressing up and making believe, but they are perfectly aware of what they are doing. It is to them just fun, not a means of escape from oppressive reality. This realism gives them an astonishing directness. They have nothing to hide and nothing to hide from. If a forest is to be burned down, they do not seek to deceive themselves about it; they accept it. They accept the unpleasant things (which are comparatively few) along with the vastly greater number of pleasant experiences.

Furthermore, there is another remarkable contrast between fairies and humans. We live our waking lives in a dense physical world in which our imagination and our emotions play a part, it is true, but a part which is constructed and restricted. Dense matter, however, does not impede the fairies. The coarsest form of matter in their bodies is more fine and tenuous than our rarest gases. In fact, it is very close to emotion, so that when they feel something, it permeates their whole body—the emotion rushes all through them. In fact, they do almost nothing but feel emotions and a sense of being alive.

Except for a few advanced types, fairies do not have a great deal of mental power. I do not mean that they are unintelligent, but they do not have to struggle to exist or even to be exquisitely happy. They do not have to worry about the things that make up the hardships of physical life, like poverty, hunger, thirst, and shelter. They do not have any need of money, nor have they anyone dependent upon them.

In consequence, their whole objective in life is very different from ours. It is true that they stand in the same relation to angels that animals do to humanity, and it is also true that animals have simple wants and are not motivated as we are. But animals live surrounded by what we call natural enemies, whereas fairies live surrounded by natural friends. So they live joyously and happily from day to day, concerning themselves with interesting occupations, and their objective is to enjoy, day by day, more and more of this fullness of life.

They are, however, very conscious of being part of a great cooperative scheme. And thus they have a feeling of certainty. The angel is always present to guide them and to stimulate them to higher development. They have a feeling of awe and reverence (but absolutely no fear) toward the angel in charge of their lives and work. I once asked one of my fairy friends who was his superior and in charge of his district, and it was amusing to watch his response. He shot up in the air a few feet to express his delight at the thought of someone so much above him and for whom he had such a friendly feeling. But also to give me an impression of his great respect, he made several profound bows, touching his head to his toes and bending double, trying to make me understand it was someone very important.

This episode will show the lightness and happiness which pervade fairy feelings, even of the reverential kind. Humans have a system of morality, which embodies a very serious attitude toward life—a moral code based upon rules and involving fear of penal ties. Of course the fairies have not the vaguest conception of what all that means. They are the truest illustration of those lovely words of Jesus: "Consider the lilies of the field; they toil not, neither do they spin. Yet Solomon in all his glory was not arrayed as one of these" [Matthew 6:28–29]. Our standards of right and wrong do not apply to these small people at all. There is no sense of good or evil in their world, only a great love of beauty and perfection. This is what every single one of them tries for: an ideal beauty in all its glory and perfection, which they strive for in everything they undertake to do. But this striving after beauty is not an effort or struggle for them but rather a constant stimulus and a tremendous joy. I think it is partly this constant inner longing for beauty which gives these creatures their sense of radiant joy. They are not to be thought of as being perfect. There may be momentary anger, and jealousy is not unknown, but it evaporates quickly. With us a negative emotion can fester in us like a poisonous discharge, but with the fairies, there are no dregs of emotion to muddy their lives.

The nearest thing to fear that they know is their feeling toward humanity. It is true that ugliness exists in their own kingdom and arouses aversion in them. For example, the water babies like to get out of the way of the deep-sea gorilla-like creatures, and these, after all, inhabit the same element and world. But while they may dislike something, they do not fear it, for they understand. There are many things about human beings, however, which are beyond their comprehension. Our motives are to them extremely strange, and they never know how we are going to react to anything; therefore, they regard us with a sense of fear, because to them we often seem so senselessly cruel in relation to the nature they love. For instance, the killing of beautiful birds and wild creatures and the suffering such creatures undergo before they die is something that shocks fairies. In nature, killing is accomplished quickly, and there is not much suffering in the process. But killing purely for pleasure, and the terror of the beasts in the process, is the peculiar horror which human beings inflict upon the fairies. Guns are something that they cannot understand, and the loud reports shock and terrify them.

I have occasionally seen fairies who have strong personal attachment for one another, mostly between individuals of the same sort, such as two water or two land fairies. The pair will go about together, work together, and be inseparable. This affection is sweet to watch, as they put their arms around one another and evince great affection. They discuss their work and show keen mutual interest in details, and they have the loveliest time playing together. Unlike animals, which reproduce themselves, fairies are brought into

being by angels. Therefore among fairies, especially those of the lower middle ranks of development,
there is nothing resembling sex, but there is a
feeling of complementary sympathy. That is, a
more positive type of fairy has a special feeling for
a more passive individual. For example, there will
be a special feeling of sympathy between an
individual oak and a neighboring birch tree; this
feeling is quite different from the way the oak
responds to its immediate kin. But these trees have
a more placid existence than the volatile fairy.
Among the latter, jealousy is not unknown. For
instance, I have known two fairies who are fond of
one another to be jealous of a third who wanted too
much attention. I remember such a case where two
green fairies had their attachment interrupted by
the intrusion of a blue fairy. One of the green
fairies came to me and complained about it. He
wanted to have the exclusive attachment of his
friend, and he exuded jealous green thoughts,
which were rather funny. At one moment he would
stalk around glowering, and the next minute
something pleasant would catch his eye which
would make him jubilant and forgetful of his
misery, whereupon he would jump into the air to
express his happiness. A fairy can seldom sustain
an emotion like jealousy for any length of time.

Eventually the blue interloper took up with someone of his own kind, and peace was restored.

I have also seen instances of fairies' jealousy of humans being expressed in different ways. For instance, in Australia I had a fairy friend whom I loved and called the Dear Little Fellow; I mentioned him in Chapter 2. As I was very fond of him, I used to talk to him exclusively. Often the fairies around him would get quite jealous because I talked only to him and seemed to take no notice of the rest. On one occasion a little green candle fairy stood off about fifteen feet, looking perfectly furious with me. He was in a rage because I had not noticed him and what he was doing, and he felt himself so superior to the other fairies of his kind that he expected a word of praise from me. He really thought rather well of himself. Many times in the garden I have admired a special flower to the exclusion of others, and the fairies responsible for the rest of the garden work have felt themselves slighted. But this sort of feeling never lasts long. In this respect fairies are very much like animals or little children in not harboring grudges.

Fairies sometimes do become pensive. For example, something may be wrong with the plants they are attending that puzzles them; then they will pause to think about it. An interesting case concerned a coffee tree which was transplanted from its native soil in Costa Rica to the garden of a friend of mine in California. Naturally, the Costa Rican fairies did not come with the tree, and so when it appeared in the garden, the fairies in California were rather puzzled by it and did not know exactly how to help this tree to its best advantage. They held a sort of solemn clinic over it. But for a long time the bush made no progress, which really worried the fairies in charge. They succeeded in getting some advice, however, and in consequence the little tree took a fresh start and did well.

As I have said, fairies function mainly on the emotional level. The focus of their attention is on the things in their special charge (and this may be largely instinctive), but they have clear feelings about all sorts of things. They lead lives that are embued with feeling rather than thought. Their whole world, and indeed the very substance of which they are made, is vital and emotional, rather than physical and logical. Therefore, it is natural that they should be as competent to *feel* as we are to shape and control physical things. On the whole, as I said before, these feelings are positive and beneficent, but sometimes an individual will get rebellious and full of wild notions, or refuse to work or even become quarrelsome with his neighbors. I know of no case of the rebellion of an entire group. The individual who makes trouble is shunned by his fellows; he is ostracized. A friend of mine observed an extreme case, where a fairy quarreled continually with a neighbor. Finally the angel who had him in charge arranged with another angel for a transfer, and the rebel was sent many miles away. He drooped for a while but got over it all and resumed his happy state. Such extreme cases must be very rare, for I have never seen one. Of course fairies are not tied to one spot or one garden, and now and then one will take it into his head to go somewhere else. It is all easy, natural, and even, to some degree, casual. A human being who keeps a fine garden, loves and cares for his trees and plants, and perhaps even has some feeling for the plants' inner life, will attract many more of the Little People than another person may do who is indifferent to this aspect.

All fairies love young things—children, rabbits, cats, fish, or trees. Youth has a special appeal to them, partly, I think, because there is a bond of sympathy, partly because both are full of joy and happiness. Children, and indeed all young things, are very open to the fairies. Fairies love little children, watch them with keen interest and delight, and even try to copy their games. The same applies to young deer and rabbits. The fairies watch for them, and I think many young creatures can see fairies, as they are, after all, closer to nature's repetitions than we are, and thus their sensibilities are not dulled. During the spring season, the fairies know every deer and rabbit and squirrel, and they try to protect them as much as they can by putting ideas into their heads and strengthening their instincts. It is a pretty sight to see a fairy enjoying the gambols of lambs, for instance, jumping around to encourage them. There is a close feeling of kinship and friendliness. One of the closest relationships exists between fairies and birds—especially young birds. They will caper about to draw attention to a worm, and if it happens to be a worm or grub that is a detriment to garden life, all the better for the fairy and so much the worse for Mr. Worm.

The point of view of the different classes of fairies—water, land, fire, and air—differs somewhat, for their interests vary. For example, the not uncommon attention which land fairies pay to humanity is almost entirely lacking in other classes. Land fairies know our (to them) unaccountable ways and have a sort of timid and doubting attitude toward us, but the others are either indifferent or curious, or even hostile. Land fairies, again, move about over large areas much less frequently than do air or water fairies. In some ways, the land beings are more self-reliant and individualistic. In fact, the difference between water and land fairies is much like the difference between animals of the water and of the land. The water fairies tend to go about in larger groups, the land fairies in smaller, and within the land group there are many quite marked personalities. A land fairy also has more imagination, and therefore wants to be more like human beings and to copy their actions, as they think us so strange and amusing. They also understand that human beings are superior to them in intellectual power.

Dominating the feelings of the fairies that inhabit the surface of the sea is the fact that rhythm, which plays so large a part in the lives of all fairies, is for them embodied in the physical rhythm of the waves. Of course each great group has a consciousness of the element in which it lives. One might say that one group has a watery feeling, another a fiery one, and so on. But each division also has something in the physical world which gives those fairies a certain character.

In the case of the water fairies, the waves give them a fine feeling of effectiveness. They are in constant movement, like the surface of the sea itself, and just as the sea is one great mass in which there is not much differentiation of material, so the fairies of the sea are a homogeneous band. Fairies of lakes have much the same central experience, and those associated with streams have the flow of the water as their basis of activity.

In the case of the beings of the air, altitude, vast distance, and a sense of almost complete freedom from physical attachment mark them. It is for this reason, perhaps, that they are so highly evolved. They are restricted neither materially nor spatially, but at the same time, they are less definite in their form and in their outlook.

Salamanders, or fire fairies, are equally independent of humanity's influence, but they are after all attached to a physical phenomenon. There is something refreshing and cleansing about the feeling of fire fairies. Because their special element is a sort of gateway between two worlds, they seem to stand on the borderland, sharing in both. It is difficult to describe their unique point of view. They see life as a constant flowing in and out of forms, and thus they are at the heart of the alchemy of nature.

Fairies as a whole have only vague conceptions, if any, about God, who (if they think at all about the subject) embodies for them the basis of the ordered universe in which they feel they live. Fairies, of course, do not undergo the kind of suffering we do, for the struggle for existence which makes up the greater part of the suffering of our human life has no counterpart in theirs. They do suffer in a minor way when things go wrong in their world, but of course that is not real suffering in our sense of the word. I do not think that they experience pain to any great extent, although they realize that it exists, since they see it in animals and other creatures. They sometimes desire to become human beings; cases of this kind have been known, and it is only thus that they sense our worries and difficulties. They admire us in many ways, and if we were kind and appreciative of their existence, they would gladly be friends.

Though fairies know little about God, they do have a rather vague but beautiful concept of high beings in the evolutionary plan, such as their own angel, who is to them the wisest and most serene being in the world.

5

EARTH FAIRIES

E arth fairies, described in general, are a group so large and complicated that I find it difficult to do justice to the subject in a single chapter. If, however, the various principal kinds are mentioned and a few specimens described in some detail, the reader will gain at least a general impression.

I must first explain that there are four main types of fairies connected with the earth. There are, first of all, surface and underground creatures. Each of these is again divided into two classes. On the surface there are fairies with physical bodies, of which tree spirits are the finest example, and fairies without physical bodies, of which the common garden or woods fairy is the best illustration. Under the surface (and of course to some extent upon it also) there are beings with physical bodies: those belonging to the great individual rocks, corresponding to the tree spirits but far less intelligent. And associated with rocks there are fairies without physical bodies, generally called gnomes. These four vast categories are quite definite: trees, woods fairies of all kinds, rocks, and gnomes. But in and upon the crust and surface of the earth there is such a wealth of subtypes and individuals that one group fades into another almost imperceptibly, with many intermediate types that partake of the character of surface and subsurface alike. I shall discuss in some detail the spirits of rocks and also identify some of the creatures that live mainly under the earth and might be called gnomes. In two subsequent chapters, one on a garden and one on the forest, I shall describe the spirits of trees and the associated woods fairies of the land surface.

But I must repeat that there is such enormous variety among the fairies of the earth that any attempt to catalog them is bound to fail. For example, living sometimes in the earth and often on its surface, according to their activities at different times, there are little brown and gold-brown beings looking something like the conventional gnome, but more pudgy. They have old faces and little beady black eyes. These are not gnomes, strictly, but they have something resembling a coat of silky fur, smooth as a seal's, all over them, and the long jaw gives the effect of a pointed beard. The woolly material that covers the head also rises into a point, so the whole head gives the effect of a double triangle. I can only say of their movements that they are angular; that is, they do not have the easy grace of most fairies. They are seen in the country-side where the earth is covered with something more than short grass. They live mostly in groups and are somewhat similar to rabbits, for they like the vibrations of the earth. They are in part the ensouling entities of clumps of growth, and in part, they act the way fairies in general do toward grow-ing things, assisting the life with vital energy which they transform and direct especially from underneath at the roots. They also have an interest in insect life, such as ants, bees, and worms.

These fairies lead a communal life and associ-ate closely with one another, discussing their work and one another and the news of the outside fairy world beyond their little patch. They have a good time generally and are also much addicted to "dressing up," parading before one another with comical gusto, laughing as much at themselves as at one another, hugging their knees, and hopping about with glee. They are very industrious and go about doing things, sometimes with the amusingly serious air of a man or woman of business. They keep a good deal to themselves and do not mix with the rest of the fairies. They have a sort of department to themselves, because they take a great interest in the activities of ants and other small creatures, helping them as much as they can. They belong to an exceedingly ancient order of fairies and have perhaps the appearance of being old for that reason. This may also account for their aloofness and clannish spirit. They look with a sort of shy curiosity upon human beings and note their habits uncomprehendingly but do not have any special feeling or liking for humankind.

There are much darker brown, almost black, creatures which live rather deeper in the earth and are about two feet or more in size. They have a somewhat lizardlike appearance, indescribably strange to behold. They are of low intelligence and live together like animals, more or less without thought. They are mysterious looking, but they have a sense of power and share with all the fairies a never-ending activity. It is practically impossible to communicate with them, as they seem to be more absorbed in their own activities than inter-ested in humans.

In a later chapter I shall say more about two kinds of fairies with connections to the Grand Canyon: one purple and fire colored, some two or three feet high; the second, brown streaked with red, about a foot high. I have never seen the larger ones anywhere else. They convey a sense of great joy and upliftment, but they are also unusually intelligent and possess a greater power of concentration than most fairies. They are one-pointed and rather remarkably determined. Their shape is also singular, being much like that of fish, which are flat and almost two-dimensional when observed from in front but fully proportioned when seen from the side. Many fairies are thin in both dimensions, but these even seem gaunt when seen from the front, for their eyes are small and close together and their shoulders and general anatomy very slender. But when seen from the side, they are of normal proportions, although their faces, which are of a reddish brown hue, are long and thin. Their work is also peculiar. They are themselves centers within the magnetic streams of the Canyon, and they redistribute the life force that pours into them.

The brown-and-red fairies of the Canyon are more properly gnomes, both in appearance and in life-style. They deal with whatever life is unique to that particular place. I am not sure myself what their work is. It is connected with some sort of growth, but what kind of growth can go on under the earth, I do not know. If rocks under pressure change their character, I would be inclined to say they are associated with that process in some way. In any case, the changes in which they are assisting are slow. They themselves move with great deliberation. They are old and slow, and their jobs require great patience. All these gnomelike fairies, having to do with rocks and earth depths, convey this feeling of being part of a most ancient order of things. Another common quality among gnomes is that they move about in groups or flocks; still another is that they like heat, and when they happen to find rain and cold above ground, they soon disappear under the earth again.

A kind of earth fairy that is almost universal is tiny, about a foot or eighteen inches high, of a golden brown or dark green color. Such fairies might suggest a mouse to humans because of their rather long ears and general air of hopping about. A variant of this variety looks like a small teddy bear, generally light brown above and dark brown below the waist. They are cheerful, indeed gay, beings of low intelligence. They go on two legs, but they move somewhat as mice do, with quick, jerky movements. They are also sociable and live in communities and are exceedingly busy with (to them) immensely important affairs. They inhabit the earth in forest areas looking after the moss, and they like to live among the roots of trees or in long grass. This variety seems to look after the life forces of aggregates of living things. They are attractive, amusing little things, rather difficult to talk to, as they do not objectify their thoughts very clearly and are too slow about perceiving our thoughts. They dart about impatiently when they have to deal with human beings. In fact, one may say that in these fairies we have found a popularly recorded figure, for they are very like the Irish leprechaun.

None of the fairies so far described are gnomes proper, but their description gives some idea of the immense complexity and wealth of earth fairy life. Nor have I even begun to describe all that goes on inside the crust of the earth. It is a fascinating and complicated place, and there are certainly a great many more unseen creatures living there than I have mentioned. To us, many are strange and even unpleasant, but I have not thought it worthwhile to discuss them, for they have little to do with human life, and we would not ordinarily get into contact with them. As one's consciousness sinks through the different strata, the earth is seen to be in truth Mother Earth—the birthplace and the source of being for countless millions of entities.

Gnomes proper live close to or actually under rocks. They have all the appearance of the gnomes of conventional fairy tales, being short, dumpy, and gray-brown in color. The limbs are of one color and the body another, which gives them the appearance of wearing a jerkin of leather. Usually the body is darker than the legs and arms. The feet are large, pointed, and not very shapely, which gives them the effect of being shod in pointed shoes. The arms, in proportion to the body, are long and strong looking, with hands which are lumpy and not very well defined. It is in the face and head that the usual gnome features appear. The space between the nose and eyes and mouth is wider than in human beings, and this gives the head a flattened, shovel-like appearance. The chin, furthermore, is exceedingly long and sharp, conveying the effect of a beard, and their heads have all the appearance of being covered with a conventional cap. I have lately studied a little group of these creatures in a clump of gigantic boulders. I must say they have a fierce appearance and no particular liking for human beings. They emerge from under rocks to peer at intruders to see what they are like. They are commonly found in the country where there are many gigantic rocks and very little else. They feel closely identified with their own surroundings and landscape. If you wonder what happens to the rock fairies or gnomes when humans excavate a quarry or in the overhangs along the highways where rock has been blasted away, they disappear.

That is all. They leave. And why not, with huge cranes moving and rumbling in and scooping out the rock, and later with cars zipping along the roads? So humans displace them.

One always sees little groups of four and five together, as they are not such individualists as are the garden fairies, for example. They have definite likes and dislikes, but their intelligence is not very high, and their emotions are of rather a primitive order. The last time I observed them, it was strange to see how these beings were attracted to me because they knew that I could see them and communicate with them when I tried. Yet at the same time they were repelled, for they did not want to be disturbed by strange things. Most fairies like novelty, but these beings have an aversion to change of any kind. It is interesting to watch them, for they are very different from most fairies, and it is fun to try to gain their confidence. Slowly, bit by bit, they get used to one and are ready to communicate a few ideas. But even these ideas are difficult to get hold of, and they deal with the obscure life around the gnomes. One of the most interesting things about them is that they regard the rocks as their friends and as living beings.

The singular thing is that the gnomes are right, for rocks are living in a true sense. They are capable at least of a faint response, strange as it may seem. Large rocks which are very old have slowly, down through the ages, gathered a kind of personality, determined by their basic constitution and their experience. When I talk about responses, I mean that such an old rock can feel, very dimly, like or dislike for a person if it sees that person a number of times. It would be better to say that a rock feels rather than sees. If a person repeatedly came and sat on a rock, the rock might feel dislike or liking. This would not necessarily happen with everyone, only with people who had some feeling within themselves of liking the rock or who have experienced some sense of communication with nature.

In Australia I had several experiences with rocks. I have always had an especially affectionate feeling for rocks, something like the feeling I might have for a cat or dog. In Sydney I had a special rock which I used to visit often, to sit by the hour overlooking the harbor. This rock used to know when I came and sat down on it, and it used to exude (if one can use that word) a feeling of pleasure which was vague yet of the same nature as what my dog felt when he had not seen me for a few weeks. It was pleasant to feel its response, as it blended in with the feeling of the sea and the trees around me. It gave me a great sense of harmony. When I got up to go, the rock felt sad, not understanding why I was leaving. It was pathetic, as the rock tried so hard to feel, and yet it was so vague. It was like a deaf and dumb person trying to be understood.

In the following passages I give the reader the experience of someone who knows much more about these things than I do. Some of these stony personages mentioned I have known myself. The writer uses the term *etheric* for the kind of matter of which fairy bodies are made and *astral* in reference to still subtler matter. The description refers to rocks observed in a great park in Australia. The first rock dealt with was on the edge of a stream, embedded in the roots of a great tree.

> An inquiry was made into the constitution of this simple being, and it was found that there is an organic arrangement in the etheric body, at least in this specimen and perhaps in others, which is the beginning of a psychological organism. The rock possesses its physical crystalline body, its etheric double and the beginning of emotion. The granitic structure is well understood by any student of mineralogy. The etheric double constitutes a counterpart in "ether," which normally occupies

the same position in space as the rock, but is slightly extensible beyond this area; the astral body is slightly more extended in space. The etheric double contains what was not before noticed—a nucleus such as is possessed physically by, say, a simple cell or other low form of vegetable or animal life. This etheric nucleus has a special value as the register of experiences, and it enables friendly folk to assist the growth and development of the rock. . . . It was found that by placing a hand upon the rock energy could be poured into it, which the rock enjoyed and utilized. This applies to surface portions of the rock's anatomy, but it was discovered that if such a stream of energy were directed into the nucleus, the force thus contributed would spread itself throughout its whole being, very much as something poured into the human body as the heart rapidly circulates with the blood throughout the whole organism.

The curious semblance of a separated personality seems not uncommon among rocks. A very cursory search has already revealed three other cases besides that above described, and no doubt many more could be found. They display unexpected differences in the strange rudimentary mineral intelligence which animates them, making one feel that a rich mine of knowledge awaits the patient explorer of these hitherto untried fields.

The rock already mentioned was distinctly friendly as far as his very limited power of expression went; he showed the germs of affection and gratitude and was evidently prepared to be responsive to the extent of his capacity. In some far-distant future he will develop into a sociable, living, devotional creature, faithful unto death in his friendships, perhaps a hero-worshiper, almost too dependent upon the object of his adoration.

Our second specimen, a rock lying by the side of an old road, now but little frequented, was a marked contrast to the first. Instead of responding to human advances, he decidedly repelled them; his attitude conveyed an unmistakable suggestion of "mind your own business and leave me alone." He was consequently less evolved than the other, but there was the beginning of strength and reserve force about him which prognosticated a future of iron determination—irrespective of the possible ferric compounds in his physical form—quite likely, however, to be marred by selfishness and unscrupulousness. It may seem fanciful to predicate such qualities of rocks; yet the seeds were so clearly present that it was not impossible to realize the promise of flower and fruit much later. We noticed that a considerable portion of this rock has been cut away in order to make the road; it is interesting to speculate as to whether this face had any connection with its misanthropic attitude.

A third case which drew our attention was a huge rock on the edge of a lofty ridge—hood-shaped, projecting like a roof over a curious little cave, which could be entered only by a rather awkward bit of climbing. Inside it was a much lower piece of roof with a large oblong hole in it; and it appears that this unusual formation had once been utilized in a very odd way. A fugitive savage, seeking to escape from the pursuit of other savages armed with spears, caught sight of this queer hiding-hole as he ran past below it, climbed up into the cave like a monkey, threw himself up through it, and thus avoided, by a fraction of a second, the murderous group of hunters, who supposed he must have fallen over the precipice. This dramatic escape was evidently the one great fact in the rock's otherwise monotonous history, and it had impressed itself upon him with such force and clearness that when an attempt was made to penetrate his consciousness he at once reproduced the scene, just as one who has passed through some tremendous experience cannot refrain from telling it in season and out of season. It seemed for a time impossible to get anything else out of him; but presently it was found that there was in him also a vague consciousness of the landscape spread out before him; it would, of course, be impossible to say that he saw it, yet it dimly impressed itself upon him, so that he might be said to feel it and to know of changes which took place in it.

The fourth rock observed had the most singular history of all. He was another of the huge hood shaped projections, but the cave under him had in very ancient times been used for human sacrifices and has still a horrible atmosphere clinging about it. Psychometrically it is easy to discover any one of the appalling scenes which the rock has witnessed, but strangely enough, none of them is as clear in his consciousness as the picture of the escape was to rock number three. One would say that he was not so good an observer! On the other hand every particle of him is permeated with a weird shuddering horror which is quite beyond description, so vague it is, and yet so deep-seated, so thoroughly engraved in him, so entirely a part of him as to seem a necessary factor in his existence. Yet there is a touch of ghastly enjoyment in it also—some strange, ancient, incomprehensible evil for which modern languages have no name. No clear consciousness of all this—nothing but a slow, dark dream of unutterable ill. Into what tragic, unearthly future can this develop, one wonders.

The foregoing stories will convey to the reader a good deal about rocks, and they have the merit of being written from the special point of view of the profound, shall I say unique, experience of the writer.

[C. W. Leadbeater and Fritz Kunz, *The Personality of Rocks*]

How fascinating is the old earth when one realizes how much more life goes on than most of us suspect! To many readers of these chapters, all this will seem strange and perhaps unbelievable. Perhaps one of the reasons most of us grow old and dull and really lose touch with the world of living things is because we cannot see the life around us and refuse to believe in anything we cannot touch with our fingers or see with our eyes. Our vision becomes thus limited, because our direct experience is bound to be small; and thus we age prematurely, and life grows monotonous. But when we try, just try, to believe and even to experience some of these things which may at first seem so strange and even mad, we recover touch with the departed glory of nature, the mother of all living things, and thus recapture youth, which is life. In my life that hidden world which I have been describing—especially my friends the trees, whose story is yet to come, and the little fairies in gardens and woods—have meant more than can be conveyed. If readers can follow the subsequent chapters not with disdain but with an effort at understanding, and if they will only try to get into touch with the life I see and have endeavored to record (even against their "better reason"), I think they may get a new happiness and a new understanding of the problems of life.

The earth on which we live is peopled with these delightful, charming, and joyous beings which I describe. Our gardens, the forests, the mountains—everywhere around us—are peopled by them, and so we live in a world where everything is thrilling with a sense of being alive. If we ourselves could fully realize it, we would have the true secret of eternal youth.

✤ 6 ✤

GARDEN FAIRIES

Among the fairies who live on the surface of the land, one of the most important kinds is associated with the woods and gardens and includes the spirits of trees. Perhaps the best way to convey the special qualities of these fairies is to describe members of each natural division: those of the garden and those of the forest.

There are several types of garden fairies. The smallest of these has the proportions of a candle and is rather feminine in appearance. They are from nine inches to a foot tall with a head a couple of inches long and a human face where the flame would be, but in coloring the body is bright apple green or yellow and the face tan. They possess hands and arms, in proportion, and just suggestions of short legs and feet. This particular fairy seems to deal with little plants that grow in borders, such as lobelia, alyssum, and masses of small plants in groups. These beings do not respond very much to creatures or events outside their immediate world; they are rather primitive in their reactions, though capable of feeling both affection and jealousy for their plants and for one another. They are avid for new sensations, for that is the way they learn. Groups of three and four are to be seen drifting about any pleasant attractive garden.

Then, among the tulips and similar flowers there is a type that is about a foot tall, much more human in appearance than "candle" fairies, but still rather like human shadows, having the outline without the substance-form in faint purple light. Some of them have delicate long faces, rather like a faun's. One would never mistake them for human beings, not only because of their diminutive stature, but because they are such quaint caricatures and look so tenuous. Their limbs are human enough, but frequent imperfection of hands and feet appear. They have a variety of fingers and toes, and some of their hands look more like the paws of a kitten. Around them is a kind of diaphanous matter that seems phosphorescent, in beautiful shades of rose and light purple.

In this particular garden that I am describing there were some lovely beds of pansies. About them floated some equally lovely and delicate beings, which remind one of butterflies and are short-lived. They are tiny things, only a few inches tall, having faces much like the pansy itself. The body is very like that of a butterfly or dragonfly—torpedo shaped and much narrower than the face. The body and head together are perhaps four to five inches long, and of this, the face is perhaps an inch. Projecting from the neck and virtually the whole length of the body are two thin winglike structures, which, however, do not fulfill the function of wings but so far as one can judge, are merely decorative. The face and body are flesh-colored but tinged with shades of mauve, violet, and purple; the wings are similarly colored, but variegated and brilliant. While I was watching, I saw four of these in only a few minutes, moving about the pansies in the window boxes. After all, in the invisible world, just as in the visible, there is a community of life, and fairies are as likely to be wherever there is a bed of flowers as a group of butterflies would be.

We now come to the common garden fairy, in many respects the true, central type of fairy. In fact, he corresponds to what most people mean by fairy when they speak of fairy life. It is he who was described in detail as a "typical" fairy in the third chapter. This particular garden fairy has a few rather big specimens, between eighteen inches and two feet tall, and in many ways quite human in appearance. They have a nose, two eyes, a mouth, and even ears, and hair rather like wool, usually of a dark brown, like the bark of a tree. The face, like that of all other fairies, does not have the same proportions as the human face, because the nose and eyes are spaced more generously. It gives them a permanently surprised look of curiosity. And, indeed, all of these fairies are exceedingly full of curiosity. The lack of eyelids and eyelashes also seems a little strange when first noticed. Their faces are golden brown, and the body, when in repose and not "dressed up," is emerald green, reminding one of the bright green beetles some-times seen in spring. They have hands and feet quite like ours, although the latter are somewhat more triangular. The whole effect is quite delight-ful. These fairies were playing among the lilacs in the garden while I observed them. As they have the highest intelligence of all their fellows in the garden, they maintain a sort of supervision over some of the lesser fairies there.

The little pond in the garden had a peculiar kind of creature which, for lack of a better term, I shall call a "spring fairy." The pond is fed by sev-eral springs, and in the particular places where this water flowed up from the earth, there were strange, long creatures, with something of a jelly-fish appearance. Their most definite part is a bluish, dimly featured head, which melts into a bluish body with very little suggestion of neck between. The body fades away into vague, wraith-like tendrils and continues down into the earth for a considerable distance. These creatures seem to draw their life from within the earth, although they are at the same time definitely connected with water. It is evident that spring water has a kind of vital freshness about it that is the source of their life. These quaint spring fairies generally hover at the place where the water emerges from the earth, their heads just out of the water, bobbing slowly up and down.

In a little glazed hothouse I found a few fairies of the butterfly variety, longer by an inch or two than others of their type and more human also, but otherwise much the same. Evidently, after a term of hothouse experience, the butterfly type has become specialized for this special contact with the work of humans in forcing plants. They are delicate and dainty beings.

There are other kinds of beings which are an integral part of the life of the garden: the trees. In the center of the garden, for instance, there was a large, handsome, free-standing, and solitary hickory tree. The aggregation of the vitality of all the living cells in the tree combines to make up the life of an entity which we might call the "tree spirit." Thus there is a being that lives, as it were, with the tree as his body, or merging with it. He is an integral part of the tree itself and cannot move about, away from the tree any distance, as the fairies can move among their shrubs. Indeed, there are no trees without tree spirits. This spirit is not always visible, for it only appears when it desires to do so. However, the consciousness of the tree can project itself externally on occasion and take form. This form, again, usually has a human semblance, but looks much more like an elongated full-size shadow of a human being, very long and very thin. Some of these tree spirits are strong individualities, but, of course, the majority are rather undistinguished. This old hickory tree was charming and delightful, and its spirit, whenever it takes form, is rather like a tall brown American Indian shape with a brown, rather barklike skin, high nose, vague hair, and two pinpoints of black for eyes. He is not exactly beautiful, but he has great charm and is exceedingly cheerful and friendly. In some ways, he gives one the feeling of a cheerful, wise old person with quite a whimsical personality.

Dawn is a busy time in the garden, as always at this time of the day a special blessing is poured out upon the world. There is an awakening of energy, and the fairies are kept busy receiving this and disseminating it. It also begins the activities of their day. At dawn, they come back from play to work once more. The fairies think of the sun as a tremendous life-giving globe of light which is the source of all life, as they derive their nourishment principally from the sun's rays. They seem to draw the rays of the sun through their bodies. This is the nearest they come to eating. Apart from deriving energy for the maintenance of their own bodies, they help to guide the energy from the sun for the plants' growth.

Fairies have a delightful relationship with trees, looking upon them as companions who are not so highly evolved as themselves, but have the special merit of being solid, substantial citizens. They like trees and think of them as respectable and worthy and fine, but at the same time they feel rather superior to them because trees cannot move about.

Fairies take a great friendly interest in all animals, and in this garden there are some widgeon, ducks, and white swans. The fairies often come down, or look down upon the water from the slope above, to watch the antics of these ducks with great delight. There is a close tie with these birds, and the fairies often move among them freely, regarding them much as we do dogs, except that they feel slightly more of a sense of equality with them. They would always try to help these birds as much as they could, and the birds respond, for like many animals, they do see the fairies.

The household dog, a big Airedale, would lie on occasion in the garden half-asleep, giving off vague, pleasant feelings, mainly associated with recollections of bones and with digging up the garden. His principal feelings of vague happiness are indicated by a pale rose color, with occasional tinges of excitement indicated by red, and the green of jealousy when he is envious of the household cat, and occasional flashes of devotional blue in response to his master or mistress. His special moods excite a certain amount of interest in the faun faces. Usually they do not take much notice of him, but I am sure that the dog sees some of them, if not all. He takes them quite for granted. Sometimes they might shy away from him if he becomes boisterous or engages in peculiar antics. But I think fairies must appear to a dog as very vague, faraway things. Fairies feel considerable empathy or pity if animals are in any unusual state of great joy or unhappiness—especially the happiness at just being alive, for this is eminently characteristic of the fairies themselves. They also feel interest when little ducklings appear on the scene after the nesting of the pond ducks. Such occasions engage their interest more than the daily life of these animals. In other words, they respond to anything to do with the creative processes in nature, in which they always take an active part. For this reason, the life of the garden fairies is quite different in the spring than in other seasons of the year.

Fairies look upon human beings with interest. For example, they always look at the owners of this garden when they go down to feed the ducks, regarding them as superior beings. In many ways, however, they merely tolerate people, because they think of them as different from themselves. But they are, nonetheless, interested and try to watch people and to understand them. Here, the family accepts the existence of fairies, and so, on the whole, they reciprocate with very friendly feelings, but of course it is seldom that people know anything about their existence. Here, they always peeped at us from the different bushes and then went back to their usual occupation, taking us as a matter of course. They liked the little baby who played about in the garden. A baby is much more akin to them than any other human beings. Since a child is spontaneous and natural and they like this quality, they looked upon him with affection.

The dawn, as I have said, is a time when the fairies start their work. They begin the day by coming together for a moment to hold a sort of friendly get-together about their work—just a moment of pouring out their joy to the world. They are so happy, and everything seems exquisitely beautiful to them. They love the feeling which the dew on the leaves draws from the plants, and delight in the response of grass and flowers to the coming of dawn. Each of the fairies hovers near the plants which are her special charges and tries to find out if there is anything wrong and how she can best help her charges—somewhat like a doctor going the rounds of her patients. This is not done in a solemn manner, however; the fairies hop about all over the flowers when things are going well, or if they are more than usually pleased with the flowers, to express their satisfaction. They show their feelings in action, and they often stay with one flower quite a while, just as though it were their baby, petting and loving it and giving it great attention. It is charming to see. Of course they do not do this all day, because they like to have several recesses from their work; when they feel so inclined they go off and gather together, just to express their joy in life. They are always moving and jumping about. At noontime they usually seem to rest a while and wander off, but it is really in the evening that they have a holiday. Then they often have gatherings that are always full of joy. Sometimes they rest, near one of their favorite flowers—resting without going to sleep.

This I think describes the fairy life of a typical garden. Of course, in great gardens in tropical lands, and in special places like horticultural experimental stations, the variations are great. But I have told enough, I hope, to show the reader that a garden seen from within is a place of a delicate and fairylike beauty which goes far beyond even the loveliness of the plant and bird life with which we are all familiar. In fact, the drifting groups of candle fairies, the fluttering grace and shimmering colors of the butterfly types, and the happy activity and gaiety of the common garden fairies make the garden a kind of wonderland. We may say, in truth, that the fairy life is the crown and perfection of a garden, helping to make it a place of rest and refreshment. The fairies are happy to work with us, to cooperate in making a spot of loveliness for mutual enjoyment. If only more human beings knew how eager the fairy kingdom is to help, gardens would be even more like fragments of heaven here on earth than they are now for most of us.

7

TREE SPIRITS

Leaving the more familiar home gardens with small plants and turning to the forest, we must note again that trees are very different from our usual ideas about them. They are living beings, just as we are, except that they possess a lesser degree of consciousness and do not react to sensation as quickly and as keenly as we do. As mentioned before, within the tree there is a tree spirit, from which it draws its life force. There is no tree, however small, without its tree spirit; the tree spirit grows with the tree and disappears with its death. This personality can emerge from the tree for a little distance when it so desires, usually assuming a form that is more or less human. When inside the tree, the form is much vaguer and practically invisible, for it really defines itself only when it projects itself outside. Most tree spirits look alike to the extent that they all seem to have a tall, brownish form which looks something like the first drawing a child makes of a human figure—square, slightly thick, and suggestive of a papoose, with little eyes and nose exactly as in a child's drawing, and hair also very like the few coarse lines drawn by a child, black and fibrous. This is, of course, a very general description of tree fairies. Different kinds of trees, such as oaks, pines, and birches, have slightly different features typical of the species, and some trees seem to have a great deal more personality than others, just as human beings do. Certain trees are unique individuals, while others have nothing that particularly distinguishes them.

While they are inside the body of the tree, tree spirits do more work, in that they look after the tree and control its energies. This is analogous to the maintenance of a human body: The tree draws its chemical nutrients from the earth, water, and air, and when these are right and plentiful, the process goes well, and the tree spirit is happy. His happiness in turn reacts upon the chemical processes within the tree and makes them more effective. It is very much like a person who eats dinner in peace and then digests it with a feeling of well being, which in turn aids digestion, just as worry impairs it—though, of course, trees never worry. When, at intervals, the spirit comes out of the tree, it is usually drawn forth for various reasons. For example, one might see a human being whom he likes and come out to look more closely at her and express his liking. Often when I have sat under a tree the spirit has come out to express its affection, though, of course, in rather vague terms. The spirit may even follow one for a few yards. At night these beings seem to have more free time and opportunity for social life. They all come out of their barks, and if the person upon whom they have bestowed their affection is staying in a house and the tree is not too far away, the tree spirits may come out and go in search of her. I think one reason why most people feel afraid at night in a forest is because all these beings seem to have emerged from their trees, so that one feels surrounded by unseen presences. Many people feel as if thousands of eyes are peering at them which, as a matter of fact, is quite true! I do not think that tree spirits would harm anyone in a forest, but their vibrations and feelings are so different from ours that it often gives us shivers up and down the spine.

It is, of course, possible for a tree to have an aversion to a person and feel dislike, and a case of this sort happened when I was a little girl. Though I cannot vouch for all the details of the story, as I did not witness the incident, I did observe the tree spirit to whom the story was ascribed. There was an ancient tree in a garden in Java whose branches were endangering a house, so some Javanese were delegated to trim it. Each time anyone went up the tree or on the roof for this purpose something happened to them—either their leg was broken by a fall or their arm was thrown out of joint. Because of all these accidents, nothing happened to the tree, for people refused to do the work. They attributed the accidents to the malignant influence of the old Kashmir nut tree spirit. I can vouch for the fact that when I was a child, I did not like to play under that tree, although I was at the same time fascinated by the strong and powerful looking old tree spirit. He did not like human beings at all, for he remembered a time when he was surrounded by trees and not by houses, and he really blamed human beings for his isolation and loneliness. When he projected himself toward people, he looked rather like a thin gray-faced ape of huge dimensions, perhaps fifteen feet tall. When within his tree, he was much taller, for it seems that the operation of densifying the body outside the tree draws the matter of his subtle vehicles into a smaller volume.

On the whole, however, trees generally feel quite affectionate toward people. In fact, they are distinctly different from garden fairies in this respect. They have the same kind of feeling of loyalty as a dog does, but they are more dignified and do not gambol and romp about as dogs do. This loyal affection is probably due to their rooted condition. An instance of this kind of affectionate response happened to be witnessed by someone besides myself and was experienced, furthermore, by dozens of others who did not quite understand what it meant.

At a school in California where we were invited to the commencement exercises of the graduating class, the children's affectionate response happened to be witnessed by dozens of others who did not quite understand what it meant. At the commencement exercises, the children performed a play about fairies. One girl, who had been very happy at the school, took the part of the spirit of a fine live oak. At a certain moment she emerged from behind the tree as though she came from within it and was to address the tree as her home in terms of affection. When she came to the words, "Dear old tree," she said them with truly sincere feeling, which was especially intense because she was going to leave. Because the play was about fairies and performed by children, and because the audience was sympathetic and attuned, when she said those words, they were an appeal to the real spirit of the tree. He responded by coming out with a rush of affection so strong that the whole audience was stirred, and many people had tears in their eyes though they did not know why. The girl who had called him out was also greatly affected. This was a clear case of the natural feeling of trees for humanity, when people are of right mind toward them. In this case, the spirit of the tree put on an appearance of a tall, benign being radiating good will. How very different from the spirit of the Kashmir nut tree!

The differences between the various kinds of tree spirits are not so marked as, say, between varieties of dogs. I have already described elsewhere the spirit of a hickory tree, so it may be of interest to give you descriptions of an oak tree, a pine, a maple, and a birch. In a small forest I have observed a beautiful oak—a kind tree, whose spirit is about fifteen feet tall with a human outline more Western or European in feature than those previously described. His face is more oval and regular, and he is better looking and more "human." In color he is dark tan, and his hair is black.

Tree spirits are slender, like elongated Burne-Jones figures. Sir Edward Coley Burne-Jones, you may recall, was a British painter of the Victorian period, much known for his pictures of fairies. Their coloring is a little darker shade than that of their bark, being a brownish gray, their hair is brown, and they have misty gray eyes. They have sweet, gentle dispositions, and their movements are rather quick and fluttery, reminiscent of the movement of the leaves of a birch tree. I have never seen any tree spirits that are not in some degree brown in color, although the variations are many, from the red-gold of the redwood trees to the gray-brown of the birch. Evidently this is the basic color type, but there is also a relation between the color of the bark and the color of the spirit in any individual tree—its color probably derives from the fiber and bark.

The pine spirit is a dark person, with rather square features and a great deal of dark green about him. He gives one the impression of being honest and frank and pours out a radiant feeling of harmony. He is not so tall—this particular specimen is perhaps ten feet—but sturdy and powerful looking, with black hair (coarse, as usual) and black eyes. He withdraws from his tree with great deliberation and gazes about in a penetrating manner. His quality is not as vigorous as that of the oak, who may be said to give a real impression of virility.

It seems that the slenderness of form that

characterizes all these spirits has some relation to the trunk of the tree and its life currents. For the spirit of a young tree is a tiny sliver of a thing, and its form enlarges as the tree itself grows bigger. (These spirits of young trees have little intelligence and come outside their barks only when older ones make it clear that it is the thing to do.) In general, a tree spirit's form is rather rounder when he is within the tree, conforming to the tree's contour. When he comes out he flattens a good deal, just as a human body is narrower through than across.

I also observed a young maple tree which grows nearby, on the edge of a wood. He displays the "American Indian" character much more than the others. His general appearance is decorative, rather like pictures of a young Indian man. Whereas the hickory tree gave an impression of a staid old Indian warrior, this maple has the springing quality of youth. His color is, in general, a yellowish brown, with variegations of rich red and yellow, evidently correlated with his autumn leaf colors. Instead of hair, he has a sort of autumn leaf headdress, which makes him look very gay, and he is quite evidently proud of this stylish effect!

The house in which I am writing this has a few trees around it, mainly birches. The woods begin close by, and it is easy to contrast the life of the scattered trees encountered in or near a city with the conditions here, where the trees near the house are practically part of the woods. The isolated hickory, cut off from his fellows, has less of the life of his own kind, in fact almost none, so he has to find his interests in human beings and animals, with the result that his mind grows more than his emotions do. Here, the woods give the trees a sense of kinship with their own kind, and thus they are more interested in what goes on among themselves than in human beings, although they feel very kindly toward people. But between the house and the edge of the wood a number of birches have lately been felled for firewood, and the rest of the trees resent it and do not feel so friendly to human beings. Trees dislike being cut down more than fairies resent their plants being destroyed, for of course, the life of the tree spirit is closely bound up in the life of the tree.

In these woods, which are fairly close to civilization, yet far wilder than a city park, there is a feeling of expectancy. The life of a tree is not at all certain, and human beings do interfere. This particular forest gives one a feeling of youth. The trees all live together and feel kindly toward one another, but they take a definite interest in the human beings around, and they consider these beings as aliens, apart from themselves. Human beings tend to think of trees as firewood or shade or decorative objects but very seldom as beautiful individuals or as anything that is at all alive. The trees feel this, and it arouses in them a close community spirit, for they realize that they are of one kind and we are another.

I should make it clear that trees react to things very slowly, and it takes them a long time to assimilate new experiences. Their understanding is limited, of course, so when we speak of them as thinking or feeling this or that, what it means is that they react in a manner which is half-somnolent in comparison with human beings. And of course there are differences among individual trees. Nevertheless, when a forest has been cut down ruthlessly, the trees that remain have strong feelings of a mixed character—injury, loss, and a sense of isolation, though at the same time there is in nature a great sense philosophic calm and the inevitability of things. Our idea of a woods is a nicely cleared place, but the ideal according to trees and fairies is a place where there are trees and a great deal of underbrush and wild life. The trees and the fairies feel a close link. There are fairies who frequent those places where underbrush and flowers and grass grow together, but if everything is too tidy, they are not attracted. Our ideals and those of the woods' life could be reconciled if we could intersperse our cleared land with large areas of wild growth. Many people may think this a sentimental point of view because (they will say) it is necessary to cut down trees in order for us to be able to live. There is, of course, some truth in this, but nevertheless, in our Western civilization we are both wasteful and ruthless, and the needs of the land and of the forest do not appeal to the average commercial person. I have been all over the northwest of the United States—at present the greatest lumber territory of the world—and I have seen miles upon miles of absolutely barren country with only the tree stumps standing. It gives one a sense of nightmare to see the burned out stumps without any signs of life, to see no fairies where once their life was rich and full, and to know that magnificent cedars, spruce, and pines were slaughtered and left to rot.

On the Pacific Highway near Vancouver there is a magnificent stand of first growth timber. When I first passed it, this was one of the most beautiful forests I had ever seen, rich with fairies and a sense of tremendous happiness. But when I passed it again, I experienced a sense of deep horror because half of those magnificent trees had been cut down, and where there was once beauty, ugliness and barrenness reigned. The feeling of the few trees that remained was one of expectant terror, looking hopelessly on and waiting to be cut down, for we must remember that trees cannot run away. This lumber company had been offered, I am told, a large sum of money, or equivalent forest elsewhere, by the government and private individuals if they would not cut down this particular forest. It was one of the rare bits of first growth timber left in that part of the world. Think of the loss to thousands of people right on the Pacific Highway who were thus cut off from passing through the very heart of such a magnificent forest!

The woods at our doorstep here in New Hampshire is characteristic of the summer growth all over the United States, except in the far West and the extreme South. The tree spirits we have described are happy in their existence and full of a sense of enjoyment. They like standing in the soil and feeling the sunshine pouring down upon them and the wind blowing through their leaves. It gives them a sensation of dancing. Trees love the wind and even a wind storm, for it offers them a kind of excitement as they keep themselves erect and steady while being swayed by the power of the storm. They do not like being blown down, but they take this philosophically, as it is to them like a battle in which one or several may be marked as victims, for to them this is a natural end of life. The rank growth round about them is alive with fairies. The animals scurry about bent on business and pleasure, and the trees take all this in, interested in the smallest details of the woods' life and feeling a happy and tender sense of protection toward all the plants and animals, for after all, the trees make it all possible.

Naturally, in a wood like this, the fairy life is particularly rich. Here are all the kinds we have seen in the garden, with slight differences because life in the woods is different from garden life. There are more varieties of fairies. There are, for example, tiny fellows about a foot tall, of a rich golden brown color, which have human outlines as vague as that of a tree spirit. Their faces look much more like little monkeys than like human beings, and they live in the mossy part of the woods, looking after small ferns and mosses. Then there are a great many of the small brown and gold variety of gnome mentioned elsewhere, as well as some lovely deep blue fairies about eighteen inches tall which flit about among the underbrush. There are also a few water fairies down in the brook. They are tiny, slender things which look like translucent pale blue water, quite human in appearance even though only ten or twelve inches tall. Freshwater fairies seem never to get so fat and roly-poly as the ones who inhabit the sea. The numerous lakes and ponds have the same kind of water fairy, but these are rather bigger, from about a foot and a half to two feet tall. But there are never so many fairies in freshwater as in the sea, which appears to be their ancient home and birthplace. Here and there in the forest are fairies almost of the standing of angels which are of human size and form, perfectly colored in yellow and green. These help to direct the woods' life. Over all, an angel is brooding—over the fairies, the trees, the hills, and streams which are part of his life and are his trust. He is a powerful personality, and the valley is just as much part of his body as the trunk of a tree is the body of a tree spirit, except that in this case, the angel has intelligence and emotions as powerful as our own, and he is as much a being as we are, if not more so. When he takes form he looks like a beautiful human being, a clean-shaven youth with fine dark hair and a powerful aquiline face, his body enveloped in a lovely apple green. His presence permeates the life of the forest and valley.

I shall close this chapter with a description of

the wonderful redwood forest in northern California—not the familiar parks of southern and central California, but the primeval growth of the northern part of the state. This is an ancient unique forest of giant redwood trees. These trees are extremely impressive, because one feels that they are so old and have seen so many ages go by that they know the secrets of life. Each one has a distinct individuality. One particular tree spirit looks like an immensely tall American Indian of red and gold, as if cast in bronze. His height, over thirty feet, is in itself very impressive! He has dark pinpoint eyes and coarse black, straggling hair, and he carries with him a tremendous feeling of power and calm and serenity of spirit as one who has seen so much of life, its changes and chances. This immense country is covered with them, and the fairies of the forest, who are somewhat strange looking, are cast in the same mold as the tree spirits. They, too, look like Indians or strange caricatures of Indians, with nut-brown faces and little black eyes and the same red-gold bodies. Even they are tall for fairies—three to four feet. Over all broods this feeling of immense antiquity. There is little variety but these two species, but of them there are a great many. The tree spirits, and even the fairies to some extent, have together reached an incredible age. Some of the trees were born one, two, and even three thousand years ago, and their life is centered in the treetops, much more than with ordinary trees. They are aloof, not only because they belong to the ages gone by but also because they are so immense. They have seen countless people pass beneath them; they have seen innumerable things be born and die, so that to them everything that exists is just passing and transient. It is very difficult to communicate with these trees because their thoughts are concerned with remote ages and happenings, and it takes time for them to become interested in new things.

The fairies, however, were glad to talk to me; they wanted to know especially about cars, for they were consumed with curiosity about the mechanism and its use. They thought it was so funny an idea for people to sit in little square boxes in order to move about, for their notion of motion is flying. They have always known that human beings walk about, and considered them slow, but cars they thought peculiar. The fairies and the trees rather resented the roads being cut through their country, even though in that particular spot the trees were not cut down to make the roads. At the same time, they were rather interested in this new (to them) civilization. Could we only imagine what the life of these trees must have been! The fairies and animals all have lived together and helped one another as far as was natural for hundreds of years, and the trees which overshadow all have had an inner social life of a strange sort.

The tree spirits used to emerge from their tops and look out over the world and communicate to each other what they observed. They told one another about the people they saw, but there was no feeling that those older races were alien, as our modern civilization is to them. People and trees understood one another in those remote times and saluted one another when they passed. This was a strange thing to observe when a scene from the past was recalled for me by one of the trees. They appreciated this intercourse with humanity in the past and were doubtful about the future, but they had learned through their thousands of years of experience that even life and death pass away, and so they await their end philosophically.

If each of us could go out into the forest and see and understand these beings, we would have a better comprehension of the spiritual power of life itself, which is, after all, the essence of religion. They are such strange, splendid, noble, aloof beings! If only I could give some idea of what it is they say and think about their past! But it is immensely difficult to convey the quality of the forest life that these tree spirits experience. They learn from the cell life within their own bark the difficulties of survival. They see the life around them and know death intimately, as the trees next to them often fall and die, struck by lightning. But just as in the case of the fairies, the trees learn through all this experience that life never dies and is never wasted. They cannot move about, and therefore we think of them as having less life experience, but that is where we are mistaken. It is not through rushing about that one learns, but from taking into oneself the experiences from without and thus feeling the pulse of life beating within. Humanity tries to escape from suffering. When it rains we seek shelter; when death comes we put away the sight of it. The trees let life beat against them and try to withstand it. Trees are the greatest realists I know, and these grand old giants are the kings of all trees.

❧ 8 ❧

MOUNTAIN FAIRIES

G ranite peaks thrusting skyward, the Rocky Mountains are a magnificent sight with their snow-covered caps. To a newcomer like me, approaching the Rockies from the eastern slope is a memorable experience. As we gradually climbed thousands of feet above sea level, we had a feeling that we were on the roof of the world, looking down upon the tops of trees far below—yet the snow-covered peaks of the Rockies towered above us. The first sensation I had when I saw this splendid sight was that I had come into the presence of mighty kings who rule a world in splendor.

There are some powerful angels in the Rockies, and they convey that sensation of regal strength—clear, clean, uplifted, and steady of vision. They are tall and stately looking and inhabit the principal peaks. They form a company, as it were, and have a likeness to one another. They have been there thousands of years, but they convey a feeling of youthful vitality, enthusiasm, and a wonderful certainty about the ultimate triumph of beauty. They are powerful, calm, and serenely joyful. Their general coloring is suggestive of snow tinted deeply with the rosy light one often sees upon it. They have about them a beauty that is Greek in quality. The features of the fairies that surround them are of exceptional interest, because the angels of the peaks deal with air fairies, snow fairies, and virtually every other variety except fire and, I daresay, they even deal with these at some great depth.

Countless tiny fairies, which may be what are called "elementals," animate the snowfields, but since the snows here last so long they have many of the features of fairies. They are between six inches and a foot high and have bodies the texture of snow rather than furry. Their faces are like interlaced triangles, so that the actual face (with dots for eyes and a mouth) is a hexagon—the points of the star sticking out like suggestions of ears. The whole shape is rather like a cocoon of snow. They have some elements of air in their makeup and also some of water. Their intelligence is small, but they have a bright, clean feeling, which is in keeping with the splendid purity of the angels.

Around the angels of the peaks there are gathered at times masses of clouds. The creatures inhabiting these clouds come and rest, as it were, upon the mountains and bathe in the atmosphere of the angels. The angels of the peaks are like beacons whose power and wisdom shine out for all kinds of beings. Among the visitors are these cloud fairies, who for the most part are clearly of the air order.

The rocks from which the range takes its name are, after all, vast masses of crystalline and metallic formation. Associated with these metals is a type of small gnome which occurs in an astonishing variety of colors—bright yellow, red, and almost black—with geometrical faces. They convey a feeling of immense age and have hard, bright, birdlike eyes, metallic, uncanny, and mysterious. They have no interest whatever in human beings, and in fact virtually never see them, for they live snug in the heart of the mountains and feel themselves protected by the angel as they go about their appointed work. On the sides of the peaks, below the snow fields, one comes upon more or less ordinary fairies; tiny butterfly sorts in gay colors and pretty-faced slender fairies in pastel shades flit about the slopes. They are of the locale, in that they seem to have the same transparent and clear quality that characterizes everything that lives fairly high up on the mountains. Lower down, of course, when one comes to cultivated land, one sees the fairies native to such places. But evidently the special character of the angels dominates the creatures of the higher levels, and there is a joyous harmony among them all.

The central Rocky peaks are special centers of spiritual power. The angels are their guardians, and they keep radiating this blessing on the world about them. It seems also that the high metal content of the rocks gives the angels some special resources of a lasting kind, an enduring power we can only call spiritual magnetism. The angels live a life peculiar to themselves in which they share experiences and plans for the future. They visit one another individually and, at intervals, all meet together. In addition to their larger plans, they have a sort of daily program that begins at sunrise, when they face the east and draw in and then send out throughout the mountainsides the renewed power of the day. The activity increases until noon, when there is a sort of momentary pause, whereupon the declining phase of their day's life and work begins, until with the setting of the sun, they assume a peaceful, subdued condition of blessing. At nightfall their duties toward the fairies and their mountains lessen, and they have time for visits and consultation with one another. They are conscious of the part they are playing under the guidance of the Continental Deva (angel) in molding America. In this they are an important factor, often consciously helping individuals as well.

The famous Blue Mountains in Australia are also rather special. The country is very old, and its invisible life is just as unique as its animals, plants, and physical characteristics. I should say here that throughout this book, my difficulty has been that I am trying to write about fairies, not angels, and yet it is impossible to keep them apart as their lives are so closely interrelated. But I shall try to accentuate the fairy aspect.

Each peak is inhabited by an angel. At the foot of a particular slope is to be found the fairy life most native to the countryside. In the case of the Blue Mountains, there is little variation, for the whole country is practically covered with one particular kind of tree—the eucalyptus—and the associated fairy life is so uniform that it would be monotonous were it not so interesting in itself. The common varieties around the base have brown faces and full, squarish, blue bodies, are two or three feet tall and slender, like fairies of this class the world over. They give one a feeling of liveliness, but also convey an impression of endurance, as if they have seen a great deal of life—rather more than most fairies—and have learned to endure more. Their intelligence is not highly developed, being somewhat sluggish but rather determined when they have decided upon some course of action. These blue beings fit very well with the strange country in which they live. It gives one such a feeling of age as to be awesome, and the atmosphere of the mountains is so strange and remote as to induce a feeling of loneliness. The mountains are like the guardians of an old fortress in an alien civilization who have stood there rooted and strong through many strange things in their day. But the thing which impresses one the most is that there is no special feeling of welcome, but rather one of endurance and watchfulness. These mountains are not at all humanized; they are still primitive nature, and one appreciates that one is in close touch with power and life, as in those savage and primitive days of what was called ancient Lemuria.

A little further up the slope there are some emerald green fellows, a bit smaller and with much more pointed faces, and these seem to be far more joyous and bright. Their vivid emerald green is in striking contrast with the dull gray-green of the trees, the dark red of the soil, and the gray of the rocks. Their movements are quick, and they remind one somewhat of the little wallabies, or small kangaroos, which abound hereabouts. These fairies do take an interest in the animals and help them along as much as possible. They peer at one curiously as one ascends the mountain. Here, as well as higher up, there are many of the gnomelike creatures which we have described before, similar to those in the Grand Canyon of Arizona, and of course one is surrounded by the benign power of the spirits of the eucalyptus trees. I saw a tree spirits slip out of his bark and peer at me. He is about seven feet tall and has a very long and, in fact, oblong face, a foot and more in length and not more than six inches wide, a sort of tan color. The body is also an oblong, silvery gray, and quite lovely. The facial features are poorly defined and the impression they convey is one of a strength which is sufficient unto itself. Still, I am very fond of the old eucalyptus tree spirits and have many good friends among them. They are very kind, with sly touches of humor, and many are the times I have put my arms around them and petted them with affection, to which they have always responded. I have often asked their advice about things, and as they are so old, their viewpoint is permeated by a philosophy of life that has endured through countless ages in difficult circumstances. Their life has not been easy, and they have gained from the struggle.

Still higher up there are some interesting fairies. They are of the same red color as the soil and have strange but beautiful faces, surrounded by a silvery mist. After passing through their lovely company, one comes to the angel of the mountain himself. He is a large person and, for an angel, has rather gaunt features with deep-set eyes of dark blue, a great and rather ponderous brow, high cheekbones, a nose of generous size, and a full mouth—the whole face one of power and beauty. His complexion is that of a tanned human skin, his body enveloped in deep blue. I stood before him rather respectfully, but naturally curious, and he responded very kindly in a manner which gave me confidence. He had a close feeling of kinship with his fairies and the animal and plant life of his domain. And he also gave me the sensation of primitive power. He looked out upon the world around him with a feeling of having stood there so long and having seen so much that he lived in his memories. These concerned the strange people who lived there thousands of years ago, the convulsions of nature that had destroyed them, and the long array of tribes and strange beings and weird fairies which had come and gone around him. There are still some of these outlandish fairies in these mountains, but the hordes he once saw have dwindled. They look half-human and half-animal, in strange hues of brown and red.

Even peaks that are not especially high but are prominent and isolated often have an angel in charge. For instance I observed one at Mt. Constitution in the San Juan Islands in Washington. This appears to be the highest point of land on an island which is fairly central in the group, and from its top there is a magnificent view over hundreds of islands on all sides. The sound in which the islands lie is ringed by several great peaks, some of them snow-clad in summer, but in this group Mt. Constitution stands isolated. The angel in charge is one of special power, remarkable in proportion to the peak. He is the guardian of all the islands and makes this point his main center; he has saturated it with his special atmosphere. He has both power and dignity and is of a steady, slow temperament, but especially marked by kindliness and wisdom. He takes a remarkable interest in human beings and has, indeed, a real fondness for them. He seems to have a certain scheme which he is working out. He wants to maintain a special atmosphere throughout the islands, and this influences his fairies. It also makes them friendly and helpful to humanity, for this is his wish. He has also established a feeling that there shall be no barriers. He has had a wonderful piece of good fortune, because a state park has been established in such a form as to take in his particular peak and a large area around it. This is an animal sanctuary in which there are many deer and other fine wild things and magnificent trees. All this gives the fairies a very good opportunity to carry out the wishes of the angel. I think also that he has managed to impress many of his ideas on the human beings in and about the peak, for his genuine friendliness toward people enables him to understand and guide them. Even human life on the islands is quiet and receptive because it is somewhat remote.

His fairies are varied at the foot of the peak, and they continue to change in nature right up to the top. One of the commonest is a delicately colored lavender woods fairy with a very pale face. This is an extremely lovely creature, dainty in her movements. A blue sort occurs more commonly higher up, and there are many others, but what is remarkable about them all is their general feeling of great friendliness. They look with shy interest on human beings who climb the mountain. Perhaps their particular delight is the deer, with which they have a close feeling of kinship. High up on the mountain are several lakes, and these are the home of particularly fine specimens of the fresh-water fairies, blue with a slight emerald tinge to it—aquamarine, I suppose—with delicate and well-proportioned human shapes which are surrounded by this diaphanous material. The sea all around the precipitous foot of the mountain brings the sea fairies of all sorts close into the picture and gives the mountain angel a wonderfully varied family.

What is remarkable about the place is that it is not only a sanctuary for animals but also a resort for fairies and even angels from the islands and the mainland. The peculiarly lovely combination of sea and mountain and lakes and forest preserve protects and creates a splendid place, and the powerful personality of the angel draws these beings. They come for counsel and change. The angel is well known throughout the neighborhood. He always makes a special effort to help human beings who come to the mountain, and I think many people feel his benign presence even if they do not know of his existence. The magnificent expanse of sea and sky, the distant mainland and snow peaks far off key up the sensitive visitor so that he has a better than usual chance to respond to the presence of this most ancient, wise, and stimulating inhabitant.

In Java the being who helped me most in childhood about some of these things of which I am writing was the angel of the great mountain. He was always encouraging bigness and steadiness, and it was he who promised that I should come to know more and more of the fairy life. He was not only the first friend of this sort I have had but has stood all through these years as a symbol of the angelic fairy attitude towards all things. His point of view had no room for meanness or littleness. Angels are all like this, but he especially showed this power of greatness. After all, contact with someone like this every day makes a deep impression on a child. His mountain stood out against the sunset nearly every night, and the cloudbanks formed behind and around the peak. After years of admiration I suddenly found myself, as it were, beside the spirit of the mountain on his own peak. He had objectified himself in response to these years of childish admiration and wonder and had made himself known to me. He was tall and indigo hued, with indigo and gold fairies clustered all about him. He radiated courage and tenacity of purpose with sincere affection and kindness. After all, a person of wisdom and majesty who has been for centuries ensouling a certain place knows intimately all the life it displays and acutely feels the thoughts and emotions of everyone in his range. The ages give them understanding, and this angel extended his field of influence to include me and poured out sustaining life to me because I had reached out in his direction.

Mountains can thus exert a tremendous uplifting influence upon one's life, as they are symbols of greatness of soul. Everyone can be inspired by mountains if they look upon them as friends.

❧ 9 ❧

WATER FAIRIES

S eas, which most of us think of as blue waves moving under the wind and deeps crowded with fish, are teeming with thousands of sea fairies, in many varieties. They belong as much to the sea as the fish do. They are water creatures and can exist permanently only in connection with water. There are many varieties and also many differences in shape and color in different waters, but in general, I have noticed three main kinds.

First of all, there are the fairies who live on the surface of the ocean in sounds and bays near land. These I have often called in my own mind "water babies," because they look like fat, round human babies, and they are the jolliest things imaginable. If one could picture a perfectly round face the size of a tea plate, virtually no neck, an almost spherical body perhaps eighteen inches in diameter, almost no feet whatever, two vague flipperlike hands with fingers more or less well articulated, the whole affair a bright blue of soft texture, with great merry eyes in a whitish face, almost no hair but

125

with a suggestion of baby fluff and faint knobs of ears, then one would have a good representation of these jolly water babies. There is some variety in coloring and size in different oceans, but these are the most common of all. They roll and tumble against one another and in the waves have the happiest of good times. They are always in groups of three or four or more, sometimes in great companies, gaily rolling and floating along the coast. They are the happiest of all the fairies I have ever seen, and they have a very kindly feeling toward human beings, whom they think rather poor sticks for being so solemn and serious. One other characteristic is that they can give us their vital energy, of which they have an overabundance, to replenish our store when it is depleted. If, when we are very tired, we could go down to the sea and deliberately try to attract some of these creatures to us and ask them for some of their vitality, I think we should feel, in a few minutes, that we have become different human beings. In Sydney, when I was tired, I used to go down to a dock by the harbor and in a few minutes be revitalized, for water babies inhabit all seashores and salt water harbors, though perhaps on the California and Florida coasts they are especially exuberant. I shall revert to this point later.

WATER FAIRIES

When one leaves the coast and moves out onto the high seas, the water babies are left behind, and fairies of the middle deeps, whose appearance and character are quite different, take their place. These are tall, from five to six or seven feet, and have a more distinctive human appearance. They are so very thin that they are almost like living skeletons, but they are not at all ugly. They have a sort of fierce beauty, gaunt but attractive, somewhat like a highbred Russian wolfhound in manner and even to some extent in appearance, for their faces, though human, are elongated, with long noses and slit mouths. They have large, deep blue eyes and seaweedy hair, blue-black in color. The face is a pale tan or beige, but the body is enveloped in an indigo blue substance that is rather like floating chiffon, waving and flowing about them. Their arms have no articulate endings, their legs are usually vague. It is difficult to describe their misty, flowing effect, and I have not done justice to them, for they are really handsome in their own way.

Their quality is also one of happiness, but it partakes of the fierce, wild, gypsy spirit of a storm at sea even when the sea is calm (although they love storms), and they sway their bodies back and forth in rhythm with the motion of the sea. They are indifferent to human beings. They do not always remain on the surface but come up from time to time from depths of ten fathoms and more to drink in the surface experience.

The third principal variety is to be found in the great depths of the oceans. They are, again, large but more unpleasant to look at, being animal-like and somewhat like the great gorillas. They give the effect of being covered with dark blue fur, although of course the material is super-physical. They certainly are the lowest of true fairies in the scale of water evolution, so far as I know. They have practically no intelligence and only primitive emotions. They are neither pretty nor pleasant. Although they are made of dense material, so that they are almost visible to the physical eye, they are rarely seen as they almost never come to the surface. They are, however, sometimes brought up by their own curiosity and by their superiors, who call them up in hordes very much as excursionists are taken to see sights, for the surface is strange to them. They are usually brought up at night and during moonlight, because they don't like the disturbances associated with bright sunlight. It was on such an occasion that I saw some. I asked the angel of a beach in Australia what they were, and he told me. I felt uncomfortable in their presence, and they glared at me in animosity. Evidently they are hostile to human beings on general principles.

On the whole, water fairies are not so intelligent as land fairies, but they have their own occupations, which are extremely difficult to explain, although I shall try. I may say that in general, first of all, when sea fairies look at the sea, they have a sensation of being part of a vast rhythmic motion. They would, of course, be aware of all the fish, plants, and other life in the sea—in fact, all the currents of life force. This means, therefore, that they would have a feeling of kinship with a great deal of life going on in a general or abstract way. The main purpose in life for a sea fairy is to do his job, whatever form it may take, which might be described as "specializing energy." The body of a sea fairy is somewhat more fluid and differently built from that of a land fairy. The heart seems to be the central organ, and he can control its beat, or whatever we wish to call its variable rhythm, which produces a feeling of pulsation. The work of sea fairies is to specialize energy by drawing it from the sun through little surface organs in their bodies and pour it out into the sea. Like other fairies, they have numerous games, but for the most part they just tumble about playfully. Each fairy has a deep admiration for his angel, and he looks forward to the meetings of his angels, for sea angels have great convocations at the full of the moon. This would be one of the chief events in their lives, for they are not very highly evolved.

These fairies, however, unconsciously perform a remarkable function in relation to the water itself. It seems that these creatures act in relation to the life in seawater as some land fairies do to plants. The latter adjust vitality in individual plants, but the sea fairies operate on the water as a whole, and, in this way, indirectly on the physical living creatures in it. Their bodies are constructed in a peculiar manner to do this work. As I said, they have a heart center like other fairies, but in addition, the surface of their bodies is covered with scores of luminous points that are subcenters connected with the heart. When the fairies move, a sort of suction is set up in these spots of light; thus vitality is drawn into their bodies. There are at least two kinds of energy involved, one from the sunlight and the other from the water. The fairy's heart center is in the nature of a mixing place for these two sorts of vital energy. Now, in the sea itself, at more or less fixed positions relative to one another, there are centers like vortices, probably magnetic, which are, of course, super-physical. At times when the fairy has absorbed far more of this mixed energy than he needs, he pours it out of his surface centers, and it is swept into the nearest of these vortices. There it is swirled around and distributed from one vortex to another by way of equalizing the charge. The fairies do this unconsciously all day long, and in this way the sea is charged with magnetism, thus helping all the creatures that live in it. The vortices have also a relation to storms at sea, which I shall try to explain later. Charging these centers is the chief job of the water babies. The surface fairies of the deep sea have the same task, but are rather more responsible, because there are fewer of the deep-sea variety to a given area. They are charged with supervision over the gorilla-like variety of the lower depths, whose main use is to give off a sort of dense energy.

In general, water fairies of lakes and streams are not so numerous as those in the sea, even in such large bodies of freshwater as the Great Lakes, although here there are a considerable number. The freshwater fairies are quite different from the sea creatures, being more delicate, more human in appearance, and more adapted in color and mobility to their habitat. Of the many kinds, I have noticed principally two sorts, namely, tiny ones in small waterfalls and brooks, perhaps eight inches to a foot high, and the larger kind, which may be up to two or three feet high. The small ones have fairly perfect human faces and figures and are again blue, but in this case a turquoise color when found in streams and rather like rainbow light when in waterfalls. Their faces are little and heart-shaped, in pleasing proportion to the body; their hands and feet are tiny, and some look decidedly feminine. They wander about on the shores at times. The larger sort are a slightly deeper blue, and their faces are not quite as human as their small relatives', but still more so than the sea sorts. Altogether they are more human as to hair and eyes, although the spacing of the eyes is not always in our proportion.

These freshwater fairies are slender, pretty, and sweet, but they are not so full of life as those found in the sea. They are much more interested in human beings, however, and they love to watch us. Like garden fairies and creatures of the woods, they love singing and can themselves make beautiful music.

Freshwater ponds and waterfalls have fairies living in them, but they are of a gentle variety who have a feeling of friendliness toward humans, children in particular. Their sense of friendliness towards the fish and other living creatures which are living in the water is a part of the feeling all of us have when we enjoy swimming or playing in and around bodies of water.

These little creatures, about one to two feet tall, have a sense of gentleness. As water has a rhythm, they respond to the rhythm and also to our music, which they enjoy hearing. When people play and sing music on the banks of rivers and lakes, the fairies really seem to gather and enjoy it immensely.

Their work is similar to that of the sea fairies, but on a small scale. As I have lived most of my life by the sea, I have not had much experience with freshwater fairies, and I daresay they would be more interesting if I had seen more of them. Large bodies of water, however, are often ensouled by a magnificent consciousness, and some of these I have carefully observed.

A place like the Mississippi River, for instance, has a distinct character. The spirit ensouling this stream is ancient and has tremendous power, and his river sprites seem to have lived longer than is usually the case with fairies of this type, although they are not so pretty as those in lakes or clear streams. The spirits inhabiting muddy water are much less human looking, but those in the Mississippi River have a tremendous feeling of the joy of living, akin to that of the sea creatures. They love to feel the sunshine on the water. These fairies enjoy movement and seem to travel up and down the river, changing places with other river fairies. Doubtless this experience of travel makes them more intelligent than most other varieties. The effect of the river soul himself, a grand old person with a spirit of mischief in him, makes his fairies more lively and like him. "Old Man River" is a good deal more than a poetic expression! He is a being who is very much alive. Although he almost never takes projected form, when he does he looks exactly as tradition suggests for other rivers, like Father Tiber. There is a great deal in these folk traditions, as primitive people live much closer to nature than we do and so know much more about it. Old Man River is a remarkable person. He gives one a sense of power and at the same time of *joie de vivre*, but his pleasure takes a form often disastrous to human interests. I happened to be right along his course during a great Mississippi flood and so witnessed some of his handiwork, and it certainly was amazing to see the power of the river relentlessly submerging thousands of acres of land. But to Old Man River this was a lark. He had a sense of expansion and freedom and a feeling that he knew a trick or two. Naturally a phenomenon of this character and magnitude is not carried out solely for his pleasure, but since a great natural discharge was necessary, why should he not have the fun of it? We must always remember that to these beings, life and death are unimportant, and this is especially true of Old Man River, who is immensely ancient and thus has seen so much of both.

Water fairies as a whole, especially sea sprites, are not interested in us. Humans do not enter the lives of sea sprites as we cannot damage the sea to any great extent. And so they have kindly feelings towards humanity insofar as we touch their lives at all. They have no feeling of shyness, as land fairies have, because the conditions of their lives do not depend upon us as do those of the land creatures. Water fairies are intensely interested in their element, which teems with life. They are kept busy attending to the thousands of different kinds of life unfolding in the sea and in freshwater.

For the fairies, the sea is divided into areas, often some miles in extent, which are smaller on the coast and larger on the high sea. Each area is inhabited and ruled like a kingdom by the spirit of that part of the sea, who is really an angel, not a fairy. Some of these angels are not particularly highly evolved, while others are gigantic in stature as well as spirit. They guide the destiny of the fairies and supervise the energy in the vortices. One usually finds that the center of the angel consciousness is in one of these vortices, from which he can radiate his own energies and supervise all the life which goes on in his territory. This being does not necessarily have to take a form, but he can do so whenever he desires. He is always perfectly beautiful and human looking, an ideal human figure, in fact, with an immense colored halo or aura around the whole form. These angels are very intelligent, and it is much easier to converse with them than with the fairies, because they can catch the drift of our thoughts, whereas with fairies one has to be clearer and much more objective. I may say that some of my best friends are certain of these sea and land angels. They are always there and always pleased to see one, and thus they are much more dependable as friends than human beings may prove to be. Some bodies of water, such as splendid harbors, have magnificent agents in charge, but these grand persons are beyond the immediate province of this book.

❧ 10 ❧

FIRE FAIRIES

Fire fairies are of two kinds. There are small ones, about three inches to two feet in height, who have no human shape, being merely foggy outlines. The tiny ones are rather like candle flames; they belong to the elemental class and are not really fairies. Some look like insects, or lizards, or beetles. They appear in little wood fires and are called into being by the rhythm of the fire, a most powerful vibration created by the sound of the fire. This rhythm is like a harmonic invocation and ceases to exist when the fire goes out. This description applies only to the lowest type of fire fairies, who exist particularly in small fires, such as hearth fires and bonfires. The large types are from five feet to fourteen feet tall; these may be called "salamanders."

The biggest salamanders live in volcanoes and are of an elongated, thin human shape, often dwindling away at the bottom. These largest ones would also be present in forest fires; the bigger the fire, the bigger the fairy. These would be attracted to the fire from some distance, not called into existence, for there are actually places which are centers for these fire spirits, and when there is a fire, they are called from there. Thus fire fairies travel about much more than other fairies, especially as there are not so many of them as there are of other kinds. Fire fairies are much more intelligent than garden fairies, but their order of being is far more remote from humanity than fairies of the earth. In fact, they have practically no relation to humanity at all. If they affect us, it is as an agency of nature, unconsciously on their part. Their only real connection with humanity is through their love of music. They come especially for such passages as Wagner's "Fire Music" in the *Ring*.

In the past, people probably had power over salamanders in the ordinary course of events, and so there was much more relationship, but always their feeling toward human beings has been one of indifference. Most fairies are at least curious, but not so the salamanders; humanity does not interest them. They are different from us and actually rather dangerous to us in many instances. We must, after all, remember that they have the power to evoke powerful emotional currents. These emotions are not evil in themselves or in the nature of the salamander, but for men and women they are dangerous, for they are exceedingly stirring. People might attain power over these fairies, but it would be unpleasant for them to have power over us, so it is well not to try to get into communication with them, except when one knows what one is about.

The fire fairies or salamanders are not exactly feared by the rest of nature, but they are held in awe. Though fire in nature plays a destructive part, destruction is never random or casual as most people think. It is, instead, intelligently guided. Fire fairies do play a part in nature, but they are themselves much more intelligent than the average fairies because they are more closely related to the angelic kingdom. They are found in the depths of the earth, but they do not remain stationary. They are constantly moving from the depths of the earth to the surface. They are in a way, therefore, a symbol of fire, as they represent this element in their own consciousness and in their being. It is impossible to convey the vitality of the element of fire in nature. It is destructive and yet a symbol of creation. Fire is mysterious to all of us in its many aspects, and the fairies of this element are unusually intelligent in our own sense of the word.

On the whole, the principal opportunities to observe salamanders are in the great conflagrations in nature, and it will perhaps be best quite simply to describe several of these.

A volcano, of course, is a magnificent sight—not only in the physical world, but also in the super-physical. Volcanoes are places of vast energy and activity. One finds here many fire spirits, ranging from seven to twelve or fourteen feet in height. The shape of their faces, though human, reminds one of the conventional pictures of Mephistopheles, but they do not give an impression of evil. They are rather handsome, as a matter of fact. These beings have faces which peer out of the flames, and their bodies, which are indeterminate, sink into the volcano and fade away into the general substance of the volcano. Then there are a few great angels of fire in the volcano who have beautiful human faces with expressions of stern aloofness. The whole place is in movement, dancing to an unheard rhythm, for these beings constantly produce music by their movement.

A volcano is an outlet for vast energies stored up in the earth—crude energy, necessary for nature's creative purposes in some way which is not clear. Those I have seen in the East Indies were active. I looked at one of these several times over a period of years and came to know the presiding genius, an angel of gigantic stature and handsome countenance. His dignity was impressive as he controlled and directed the mighty, subtle forces that parallel the equally mighty physical forces of the eruptions. After all, only the crust of the earth sustains life, and the crust is thin. For hundreds of miles beneath there is no ordinary physical life, and so when these immense reservoirs of elemental energy are loosed upon the earth, guidance is necessary. The great angel, his fellows, and his helpers see to this. The elemental energy is not complex; the lesser salamanders use the coarser elements, and the angels transmute the finer. It is necessary for them to pass the currents through their own bodies, so the work needs concentration. Therefore, the power and dignity of the presiding angel are natural enough, for he has a great and difficult work in hand. Of course, at the same time, this is great fun, and they all enjoy the movement and the music and leaping flames with an intensity that is beautiful to watch. I was once close to another volcano in Java, a smaller one set in desert sands. Here human worship had gone on at one time, and so the salamanders took more interest in human beings than most volcanic fairies would. They looked at our party and tried to evoke from the human beings some sort of response to make them have a feeling of being as alive as they were.

This sometimes can have unpleasant effects, since after all, our feelings are very different from theirs, and thus we humans might react in a not altogether pleasant manner.

In a forest fire the beginnings naturally are small, and at first, as in any other fire, there are only a few of the lizardlike, temporary fire creatures. But slowly, as the fire gets bigger and the trees catch, a call goes out for the bigger ones, and they come sweeping in with a feeling of joy, dancing and leaping into the flames, mixing with the small creatures who are the ones who actually ensoul the flames. Most of the woods fairies run away from a fire. They try to help animals and other creatures as much as possible; but they cannot do much, and so they run away until such a time as the fire is more or less over. If the great trees are actually burnt, they, of course, die, but the tree spirits try to withdraw within the tree trunk as much as possible and protect the life of the tree. They all naturally feel that the fire creatures are not their friends, but in the fairy kingdom the tragic sense is not the same as ours. Of course, the forest fairies do feel sad when they see the plants all burnt, because so much love and work has gone into them. But as they are realists, they start the work of rebuilding right away, working extra hard since it is difficult to start the life going in the charred remains. They hunt out the little wisps of life and nurse them. As the forest fire dies down, the salamanders troop off.

Where do they go? The answer to this is rather interesting.

When I was at the Grand Canyon in Arizona I saw what was to me something unique. The Canyon is inhabited by a huge angel, not only of magnificent proportions in form, but a noble and splendid person spiritually, fitted in every way to the singular nature of the place. His physical body is the Canyon; that is, his consciousness embraces the whole chasm—its two hundred miles of length and thirteen of width and much more than its mile in depth. He ensouls and broods over the whole region. When he objectifies himself, he has a beautiful and majestic human form about thirty feet tall, with dark hair and eyes, which is enveloped, as it were, in glowing garments of light. He has many lesser angels to help him in his task, but he is in command of it all. Under him are some fairies that I have never seen anywhere else. They are about two to three feet or more in height. They have strange faces and are clothed in shimmering light of purple and fire. Most of these live a little beneath the ground, while others roam about the

Canyon, rising also above the rim. Another sort of being is individually smaller, perhaps only a foot or so tall, brown streaked with red, with a half-human face and body. These live within the earth and are rather close to the classical description of gnomes, being bent over like little old men. Their pointed faces could be mistaken for beards. Far beneath the bed of the river itself there is still another kind of being, fire fairies, the large salamanders, in what we might call a grotto of fire.

There definitely seems to be a center here of pure subterranean energy, something like that in a volcano but different in its purpose. The angel of the Canyon is himself a being who is of this nature and gives off a pure elemental power. He guards over the work that goes on throughout the entire Canyon; being himself of its essence, he can understand and protect it. The work itself is done by certain other angels who are similar in appearance to volcano angels, but are much finer and higher beings.

From the grotto where the mighty fire angels are to be seen, luminous streams of energy pour up into and through the body of the angel of the Canyon. These radiate to all parts of the Canyon and far beyond. These streams, however, are only the excess of vital forces whose main use is seen in the grotto itself. There the great fire angels take from the bowels of the earth the elemental force of the earth, permit it to swirl about in their bodies, and then pour it out into a common reservoir. From this it is drawn as required by such angels as are assisting in the coming into being of fire fairies or salamanders. The angels so engaged set up a rhythm and by its means draw out the energy they require. They mold it into form by their thoughts, and then with a sort of sudden special rhythm (which would be called a *mantram* in India) they invoke life into the creature they have thus molded and energized. With that act, the fairies of the fire come into being. Generally, two angels concentrate on the creation of a salamander; the salamanders are thus the essence of fire. They do not remain here, of course, but move to those points on the surface of the earth or beneath it where there are streams of vulcanism—volcanoes—or sudden great fires. They are the spirit of the intense heat of the lower depths of the earth and are happy only where great displays of fire are to be seen.

Nothing I can say here can convey the tremendous feeling of being alive which emanates from this strange subterranean workshop. The whole place is so wonderful and marvelous—here is life in the depths of the earth! And yet our whole universe, teeming with all kinds of life, is truly full of wonder, and marvelous.

༜ 11 ༜

AIR FAIRIES

In the case of fairies observed in the air, it is necessary to distinguish between two general classes. One class is a large but mixed group that may be properly called "air fairies," because the air is their only natural element; the other is a large but more or less homogeneous group not restricted to air. The latter are not air fairies in the strictest sense, but are rather the great crowd of highly developed creatures that have evolved from earth and water and even fire experience and are now released from these special conditions because their intelligence has outgrown them. These interesting beings have been called "sylphs." I shall use the name because it is convenient and, for once, not misleading. I shall describe sylphs in detail later, but for the moment, it is enough to say that they are quite a distinct class, of high intelligence, general usefulness, and varied origin.

Air fairies proper are of three general types. They are by nature part water and part air. The first kind live and have their being in masses in clouds;

their size varies, but on the whole they are large, loosely knit, bulky forms with slim, more or less human faces and cloudlike hair thinly streaming behind them. Their whole texture is cloudlike. Instead of "dressing up" as land fairies do, it seems that their way of playing and growing is by molding masses of clouds into all sorts of shapes. The cloud spirits are the sculptors of the fairy world, and they get a sense of achievement from floating about with their clouds and molding them. They are eager to work on suggestions from others. If a cloud mass is regarded as a living thing, it becomes a game, especially for children, to try to think it into a shape. If a child thinks hard enough of the fairy behind the cloud, the fairy will respond to the game and try to make the wanted form. It is no good trying to impose one's will upon them, for they are very elusive, but they respond to the spirit of play. Their intelligence is not great, but their function in nature is important; they have a kind of directive power over small cloud formations, and they help to accumulate the great masses for rainfall. When the clouds vanish, they retreat to mountain lakes, mist, and the sea. They are kindly beings, as all the air spirits seem to be. Sometimes the cloud spirits have delicate pastel shades around them, and when they glide about and play with one another, it is often a pretty sight. They are as serious about building their cloud forms as a child is intent on building his castles of blocks or sand. They also rather like the sensation of swooping down on a high wind with rain in a summer thunderstorm. Cloud spirits particularly love sunset and sunrise, because the sun shining through their clouds creates lovely effects. They admire such sunrises and sunsets for the effects that are created in their world. If we respond to a beautiful sunset, they will often especially try to make their show more beautiful than it would otherwise be. I particularly remember sunsets in the tropical East as a child and how, enthralled, I used to watch the display and try to get in touch with the beings behind it. I still enjoy the antics of cloud fairies, but after years of watching, I still do not understand their complicated relationship to natural displays of rain, snow, and kindred phenomena.

Probably the most characteristic air fairy is the one that is associated with storms. They are small, some four or five feet high, but shapely and beautiful. They are well proportioned according to the human model, with faces that are weirdly narrow, framed by streaming hair. Their principal coloring is like a silver birch, but with faint lights of pale blue and violet. There are generally some storm fairies about, because there is usually some wind blowing, but their relation to wind is not as intimate as that of cloud fairies to clouds. They seldom come down to earth level and are seen mainly in great troops high up in the sky. When a strong wind blows, however, they descend to the earth or ocean surface. They have an intelligence of a high order and are, in fact, close to the sylphs in nature. Storm fairies, like all other fairies, work under the direction of angels. Their superiors are a special group of angels associated with storms, and when a great storm is about to break, they are rallied for it. Just as rainstorms are high spots in the lives of cloud fairies, and other fairies have their special pleasures and events, so the windstorm is the great joy of these particular fairies. They sweep over the top of a forest in the wind, over the surface of the earth, and are to be seen normally only around great peaks in high mountains. They are the superiors of the cloud fairies and direct them.

At immensely high altitudes can be found the last sort of air spirits with which I have any acquaintance. They are prodigious monsters, floating along like dragons. I find it difficult to conjecture their length, but they are huge and have a scaly appearance. They are quite reminiscent of a traditional Chinese dragon, with a huge head, long body and tail, and big eyes. They run to all sorts of colors, and these are quite vivid and deep. What their business is exactly I do not know. Their intelligence is clearly low, but they are nevertheless centers of energy or power of some sort which has an electric quality. They float idly across the sky, but very high above any cloud level, and probably they are really moving rapidly. Storm fairies draw energy from them for some purposes of their own. It may sound absurd, but the fact is that they are like immense, prehistoric cows in the field of the sky, wandering about and shepherded to some extent for some purpose connected with the energy they possess. They never descend to the lower atmosphere and are well above all storm levels. They are interesting because they are strange, but I cannot make very much out of them.

Sir Arthur Conan Doyle once wrote a story called "The Horror of the Heights," which is suggestive of these creatures. As one of them goes floating past far overhead, it is possible to get into some sort of touch with him, but beyond a general feeling, I am unable to get anything like an idea or emotional response out of these air dragons directly. However, an angel told me that these dragons were mainly used as reservoirs of energy which the angels and fairies drew from in their work, and thus they affected the weather to some extent.

The cloud fairy seems to be partly of the water category. The dragons are true enough air spirits and, of course, storm fairies are really airy in character. But the most definite creatures of the airy kingdom are the sylphs. These are the highest type of fairy to be found anywhere and are very lovely to look at and to know. They have perfect human features and form, with beautiful, childlike faces, except that they are far lovelier than the average human being. An opalescent mist, gorgeous to behold, surrounds them. They look like human beings enveloped in this shining matter, which gives the impression of opals under sunlight, all in the most delicate shades. Their bodies are made of much finer stuff than that of any other fairies, so that it would be more difficult for the average person to see them. But, on the other hand, their intelligence is far superior to other kinds of fairies, and so it is much easier to communicate with them, for they can read our thoughts. Thus no great effort is necessary for us to understand them, and they us. In fact, many of them are superior to an average human being in understanding. Another feature is that they are not bound to any location or kind of work and so can go where they like and do varied jobs.

The ambition of the sylph is to become an angel. They are almost that, and with a little more effort, they individualize and rank as angels when they next take form. They try to achieve this goal by staying close to angels and by being of as much service as possible to the angels around them and even to humanity. It is through service and an understanding of the work of the angels that they attain the higher level. What usually happens is that they become the assistants of some angel and learn to be of special service to him; they perform certain specific tasks that he assigns to them and also act as his messengers or personal aides. Thus many angels have several of the sylphs attached to them. In this way the fairy gains in experience and also in affection, and the latter is important. The angel tries to bring out all the latent love in his companions. The relation is one of delicate tenderness, for the fairy is exceedingly happy in the angel's service and is often proud of his post. Indeed he is, in the purest and truest sense of the words, "in love" with his angelic chief, and the relation is one of such delicacy as to be almost indescribable to human beings in whom this emotion has always some residuum of physical attraction. He is, furthermore, permanently in love—another great difference!

Some sylphs have much to do with human beings. Frequently part of their work is to help those in pain and even to save people from death. They often act as guardian angels to people and tell them what is ahead of them. They are also often to be found in hospitals, particularly near the dying. One of their joys is to assist children who have just passed over and feel lost and strange. They play with them and tell them the most wonderful fairy tales and also show them beautiful games and take them to lovely places. They delight in this work with children, as they, in common with that entire world, love young things above all. Such children look forward to the return of their fairy visitors with intense anticipation.

In medieval books one reads of sylphs in the service of magicians and, however superstitious this may sound, it is indeed true. They frequently serve human beings instead of angels, and they get their experience in this relation instead of the more usual one. Ariel in Shakespeare's *The Tempest* is far more than a poetic invention. In fact, in all the literature that I know this characterization is the closest description of a sylph available. The characterization of Ariel as being bound to his master by mingled respect and love, his spirit of mischief, of his quick and adroit actions backed by the power of Prospero, his tolerant attitude toward all beings, his control of the lumpish Caliban, his command of the elements—all this shows the knowledge of the poet to be as sound here as in those fields where his knowledge is accepted as sure.

The sylphidae make the kingdom of air especially lovely. Their feelings of gracious service and loyal devotion are so delicate, their perceptions so keen, so gay and light-hearted, their spirit of mischief so pronounced, that they mark out the air fairy as unique. Water has a joy of its own, fire is strangely wonderful, but only the air supplies these heavenly creatures with their shrewd and affectionate understanding of humanity, combined with angelic power.

Another feature of the airy kingdom is that it has no physical life on which to base itself. After all, the surface fairies of land and water are concerned with a teeming physical life: even the rocks are alive to the fairies, and the deep sea is crowded. But the air is a place of vast freedom. Hence the feeling is one of less congestion and of less order and organization. Immense territories in the sky are almost entirely without population. Near the earth the sylphs abide and roam about as they need. Much higher, the sparse population of the clouds and the storm fairies appear at times. And finally, at a great distance, the occasional dragon of the higher levels roams miles above us—such is the element which has always and rightly been the synonym for all that is free.

✻ 12 ✻

THE HURRICANE

When I was in Miami, Florida, in the nineteen twenties, it was not long after two hurricanes roared through that state. At that time I asked the angel of the sea to describe this event. He did so by giving me a great number of mental pictures combined with feeling. There is only one difficulty in communicating with an angel. What he considers to be one idea is to us about twenty, and thus it takes a long time to digest what he expresses. One gets mixed up very easily, because one is always behind him in grasping his ideas. The scene opened with the Bay of Biscayne (the angel's country) beautiful under a sunny sky, in tropical peace. The angel and his fairies were going about their ordinary daily business, serenely and joyously. This was a day or two before the hurricane arrived.

I should explain that there is a hierarchy of angels, or devas, in general and, in this case, of sea angels. The immediate neighbors of the angel of the bay are his equals and colleagues. But superior to all of these, and supervising a vast extent of sea, is a still greater being. As I have previously described, in each territory ruled by angels—like the one inhabiting the bay—there is a vortex which is the principle seat of the angel's consciousness. This center is in a particular place and may be regarded as the heart of his area. There are similar vortices in the air, not so numerous, which serve air angels in a like manner. It is the discharge of energy and polarity between an air vortex and a sea vortex that results in various kinds of storms. Thus there is a constant exchange of energies between sea angels and those in the air. In fact, the whole balance of the energies of nature is in the keeping of this host. Their bodies are the seat of and indicate the flow and discharge of energy. A certain—probably small—number of exalted angels direct the course of nature in this way throughout the whole world, keeping the power of nature in balance. Our friend, the angel of the Bay of Biscayne, is thus a unit in this vast network of superior and lesser beings. The very highest ranks, because they are the immediate agents, have the power of planning the future far ahead and of knowing events of the minutest kind which we have always attributed to God. Indeed, they "mark even a sparrow's fall."

At times there seems to be too much energy

concentrated in, let us say, the tropical zone, and it becomes necessary to free it. A hurricane or some other outburst of nature's energies then results. It does not, however, occur blindly or haphazardly, but according to a splendid order which I shall now describe, reverting to this particular case of the wind which struck Miami. I must emphasize that I am describing it from the point of view of a sea angel and according to his special outlook. The following description of the preparations and the carrying out of the event is my understanding of his narrative.

The great angels who keep nature's energies in balance decided that there should be a discharge in the country covered by the storm. They indicated the starting point and the general territory, and then they appointed an angel to take charge of the storm, to prepare its details and to see it through to the end. The beginning was determined by the fact that at a certain point there was something out of balance which required immediate attention. The hurricane angel himself who was chosen for the job is about twenty feet in height, and one would think he was surrounded by lightning and dressed in garments of electricity. One can imagine him as the image of Zeus with thunderbolts described in Greek mythology. He has a powerful face with shining gray eyes and fair hair, magnificent to look upon. It gives one a feeling of awe to be in the presence of so much power. These storm angels are rare, as they do not belong to any special region but travel about the earth with the storms. They are highly evolved and have a perfect steadiness and clarity of vision that is mathematical in its precision. The Bay of Biscayne angel himself stands in awe of the hurricane angel and made this very plain to me. The hurricane angel began by selecting a couple of angels to help him in this work; these are somewhat similar to him in appearance, but smaller and not of the same level of development. In addition, a few other angels accompanied him as colleagues. These I can only call the angels of life and death, for they went with the hurricane angel in order to supervise the human aspect of the storm, as it were—the effects of the hurricane upon humanity.

As I said before, the angel of the bay had had informal advice that a hurricane was impending, and his picture of the discussion by the angels around him was rather amusing. He showed me angels talking together about the coming storm, wondering exactly how it would affect each one of them. The bay angel has a rich artistic sense and a certain rollicking quality like Irish humor, and his portraits of these gossipy conferences were delightfully lifelike and picturesque.

But the official notification was striking in the extreme. The hurricane angel first warned the angels of air and sea who were located at the point of origin of the storm. He gave instructions for them to prepare for the storm by drawing in their forces to be ready to discharge them when the time came. He gave them a definite time which he had fixed a few hours before; and with this order to the angels about the starting point, he sent out a wave of notification to angels all along the line of the hurricane's progress which he and his colleagues had finally determined. This was accomplished by having the word passed from the angels of the starting point to their neighbors down the line, until finally our bay angel received definite notice from "headquarters." He immediately began his preparation under the general supervision of his territorial superiors, for his official notice was only a matter of a few hours. He called a mass meeting of his fairies and explained what was to happen to them, as far as they could understand. Then he began to draw power into his vortex, accumulating energy. His position in the whole was important, because he was at the edge of the land. Neighbors in the sea even poured energy into him. As the hour of the storm came nearer, he increased his preparations, working them up to a higher and higher pitch of intensity with increasing power. Leaving him for the moment, let us go back to the point of origin of the storm.

At the hour set, the hurricane angel appeared with his company. He then sent out a call, ringing much like an old trumpet call to battle. At the sound, a sort of shock went through the selected line of angels all the way from the storm's starting point along its track to its terminal point. All the angels along that line became interlocked, merged in the consciousness of the hurricane angel. There are special storm fairies of the air order, and a second effect of this trumpet call was that hundreds of them swept in from all quarters. And with the call the angel discharged energy into the track assigned for the storm, personally contributing to it. This was instantly accompanied by a discharge of the excess energy of the air and water angels at the point of origin. And then, like a huge ball of flame filled with a troop of angels and fairies, the whole centering around the hurricane angel, the storm swept on its appointed way. As it approached each vortex in air and water, the local preparations were coming to a climax. With the actual arrival of the hurricane angel, these reserves of local vortex energy were discharged into the storm center, and it swept on to the next vortex stronger and more powerful than before.

The fairies working under the bay angel also added their bit. The whole thing was fun for them; they would shoot into the air when the storm center came into their own vortex and try gleefully to hang on to the storm and travel with it, shooting in their own small contributions of energy and then tumbling back into the water. Some succeeded in traveling further than others and found their way back to their proper places only after some time. Of course after the storm had passed they had extra work to do, but they enjoyed immensely the stimulation and sensations engendered by the hurricane.

When the storm hit our angel of the bay, he was ready. His particular role was to draw in his forces, as previously described, but he also had to be more than usually busy directing the work because the hurricane, at his point, had to deliver its charge on the land. When the hurricane angel arrived, the tremendous release of forces involved in the sea meeting was momentarily overwhelming and then, being repulsed by the shore line, produced such a shock that the whole organization of the bay angel was for the moment disrupted. The fairies had been expecting this to happen, and they were on tiptoe, eager for the storm to strike them. Yet, when the actual moment came, the impact was so terrific that they were thrown back and out of the path of the hurricane for a moment. They recovered quickly, however, and joined in the storm, throwing in their energy and going with the disturbances as it struck the land.

The land angel of the Miami shore, of course, knew also what was impending, but his part was passive, as he could do nothing to prevent it and understood it was his fate to have this come upon him. He did not enjoy it especially, as land angels dislike the destruction of plants and trees; moreover, in this case human beings were also involved. For we must remember that while a storm may rage on the sea and leave it virtually unharmed, on land it does much damage; time and care are needed for plants and life generally to recover their growth. Thus, when the storm hit the land, the angel of the hurricane took special care in directing his work, because so many more compli-cated life forms were involved. The angels of life and death who accompanied him took note of what had to be done and did their share of the work as the storm took its toll in their department of human life. It seems incredible, unless one sees it from within, that in the midst of all this turmoil order reigns. Yet we must remember that the hurricane angel is not only a personage of magnificent intelligence, but that cooperation, organization, and order are the very things in which the angelic host excels. Naturally, the angel of the land tried to save as much of his own charge as he could, trees and animals especially. His fairies cooperated with him in this, by jumping on a stray animal here and a casual bird there and suddenly reinforcing its instinct so that it ran to safety with a display of intelligence unusual to it. In the case of trees, all that the fairies can do is encourage them to endure. All during the storm, the angel of the Miami area gave off strong waves of steadiness to people as well as to his fairies. He is a large, calm person anyway, and he has a sense of enjoyment in living, for the country in his charge and its climate encourage this. He feels rather kindly toward Miami, because he appreciates the fact that its growth means indirectly more farms and fruit orchards, all of which involve life and experiment and opportunity for him and his fairies. He does not like the fever of a boom, or uncontrolled land development, because this means wanton destruction to the land, and this, like the useless destruction of forests in the Northwest, is resented. The angels do not mind intelligent thinning of forests, for this is constructive experimenting which contributes to the life of the whole, however much the individual tree may feel his passing. The hurricane was to the Miami angel something halfway between the wholesale and unintelligent destruction by humans and the ordered change of nature. But he accepted it naturally, as it came from his superiors.

The sea fairies, because there was such an excessive charge in their power, rushed at the land; the physical disturbance which accompanied this shock took whole sections away in some places and piled deep sand and debris elsewhere. Therefore, the sea fairies had a lot of work to do. It must be admitted that they enjoyed it, because it was a change for them. It meant that in some places they had more territory to look after and in others less, so it all made for variety.

While the storm lasted, the sea fairies were carried over the land, some penetrating several miles from the shore, an unusual state of affairs which they of course considered a novel experience. After a few hours they straggled back as the storm left Miami on its rush inland and the sea began to calm down to its normal state. For a few days, the fairies were busy reconstructing their

lines of communication and recuperating generally, but many of them came to the shore to help the
land angel renew the work of growth. The Miami
angel was somewhat depleted of his energies, and
so the sea fairies kindly cooperated as much as
possible, for they really prefer everything to be
normal, even though they are stirred while the
storm lasts.

The whole hurricane went on its appointed
way and slowly died out; as it diminished, the
storm angel left it with his storm fairies, until such
time in the future when his services would again be
required somewhere. Slowly everything returned
to normal over the whole path of the hurricane,
although of course it takes many years to make
good all the land damage.

Human beings will inevitably think that the
water fairies, sea angels, and especially the angel of
the hurricane himself are bad or evil, because to us
they have been destroying life. But this is not so.
They have destroyed forms, but they have not
destroyed the life within the forms, for life cannot
die. Moreover, these beings have performed their
function in accordance with natural law. People
destroy property, one another, and the whole face
of nature in times of war or for personal gain, and
they read their own motives into nature. But

nature has no personal feelings. All this destruction is accomplished impersonally, and even, strange to say, with a feeling of love, because the host of angels and fairies never want to kill anything and try to save as much as possible. How different from war, where we try to destroy everything! But the angels have to obey the law of nature whether they want to or not. It is their work in life; it is the very essence of their nature. Also, they do not look upon death as something unknown, terrible, and final, as we do. To them, death is but the destruction of form; life is never wasted as it goes back to its mainstream and source. It will return to take another form and thus gain new experience in this world, and experience is the keynote of all.

❧ EPILOGUE ☙
PRESENT CONDITIONS

Coming back to this manuscript after all this time, and in the intervening years having been caught up in many pursuits with a different emphasis in my main interests, refreshes for me many of the impressions that were the basis for what I wrote down so many years ago.

Even if the emphasis of my study has changed in the intervening years, I nonetheless have kept a direct, open link with these beings whom I have described in this book. In all my wide travels, the first thing I automatically do is to establish communication with the angels and fairies in whatever place I go. Thus I get a feeling of unity with the inhabiting intelligences everywhere, in every place.

When it was decided to look at this old manuscript and publish it, friends suggested that the fairy world must have undergone tremendous changes in the interim, just as our own physical world has. Certainly it was an interesting thought, but it was not until they suggested that I go back to some of the same places and see what effect our polluting of the environment has had on the fairy world that I even considered it.

Of course, it was not possible for me to travel all the way to Australia or Java or India to make comparisons, but it was possible for me to revisit the sound on the East Coast here in the United States. I did just that. These days of oil slicks, dumping garbage into the ocean, carbon monoxide fumes from automobiles, and our constant building and expansion, which takes over the land and encroaches on the area inhabited by the fairies, must have made some impact, but we would see.

It had been many years since I had gone to the particular beach that I chose to visit one beautiful, cold winter day. The sound is near a populated area, but it runs out into the open sea. From the beach one can observe both the sound and the sea at the same time. About fifteen years had passed since the time when I used to visit this beach frequently, but it was still very familiar to me. In the summer months it is densely populated with sunbathers, but in the winter very few people brave the winds.

The first thing I noticed as I watched the waves wash ashore onto the beach was that there were fewer water babies and fewer fairies. It also appeared that they no longer followed the waves so far up onto the beach but stayed on the outer periphery and went back and forth in the surf there. They enjoyed themselves and rollicked about, of course, but sadly, I must report that they are much fewer in numbers now.

The whole network of energy did not seem to be so bright or strong. This is the network of energy on the sea floor that I described earlier. It now seems strange. It appears to be frayed in certain parts, and this consequently brings about a certain disharmony in the overall flow of energy.

Another noticeable difference is that whereas in earlier years there seemed to be a symbiosis between the sea and the air, that appears now not to be working, or at least not working fully. In places where some of the patterns in the air and sea are damaged, the energy currents do not appear to be working harmoniously. I believe that the water babies do not and cannot understand very well all this pollution. It seems that the pollution in the sound (which has always existed to some extent) is more extensive now, and it extends deeper into the sea, where before it was more superficial. The oil slick from a recent tanker wreck has bewildered these local creatures. They know that there is more dirt, more pollution in the physical aspect of the sea, and they rightly perceive that this has some relation to humankind. Yet, they do not really quite understand why it is, nor do they understand why the fish are not so plentiful. They still work, but the results are not so pleasing or effective, and since they think it has something to do with human beings, they do not seem to be quite so interested in us. There is a certain tendency toward fear and withdrawal. So many of the fish and other forms of ocean life have now moved out farther from the shore. Of course my visit occurred during the extreme cold of a hard winter, and seasonal conditions have their own effect. But the fairies still feel that people have been responsible for the diminution of life forms, and so even the sea fairies are not so friendly to human beings.

Even farther out, in the deep water, there is now less life than before. The broken, discontinuous pattern of energy is evident as far from the shore as I could see. This damage is due to a physical cause, so the fairies can only partially repair the damage. Since the symbiotic relationship between the sea and the air extending over the entire earth is disrupted, there may be more far-reaching effects in the long run than I could detect in this one locale.

The air fairies can escape the effects of pollution relatively easily by rising higher into the sky. Yet they are not happy either. There is a kind of pall in the energy pattern even in the top layer of the air. The air fairies too are somewhat withdrawn from human beings and do not seem to be working effectively against pollution. Both air and sea fairies do not appear to enjoy having many people about. They are carrying on, of course, but there is a difference. They feel they can't handle—keep up with—what we are doing; they feel that this is something they simply cannot adapt to, and they get discouraged. Apparently these are responses more to air than to water pollution, for the deep water out at sea is still the least polluted of all. The deep ocean rejuvenates. I don't want to mislead you: the fairies are still beautiful and still very much themselves. And there is still a wonderful, cleansing quality to the sea.

The angels, being so much higher, are somewhat removed from the pollution, but deeply affected by its consequences. The angels are more resigned to the effects of pollution than are the fairies. They feel that in the long run, humans will do something to remedy the condition but that there is a dangerous period to go through, a period of great stress which is evidenced by a tremendous pressure in the inner worlds. And of course, devas, as a whole, have a longer-range view than do the fairies, who work for harmony from day to day.

This period of stress and lack of coherent

energy patterns is already evident from the breaks near shore of the symbiotic network that I mentioned. Pollution on the sound is sometimes very thick, and during these times of pollution alert, it seems as if there is a sort of string of (for the lack of a better word) dense energy which unsettles the reciprocal relationship between earth, air, and water. The fairies and water babies try to do something to offset this effect, but at present they are rather nonplussed and don't seem to know what they can do. The devas, being farther from it and seeing things from a larger view, feel that it will be overcome and seemingly wait for the humans to repair their own damage.

In times of pollution alert, the air fairies escape to a higher level where they are freer, but the poor water fairies along the beach, even though they could go further out into the open sea, are not as happy out there. They do not like the great depths as much as the shallows they are used to living in. These shore fairies are associated more with the land and with animals, plants, and even people with their children and pets.

So, the fairies in general still carry out their work, but on the whole they do not feel so related to human beings, except when both humans and fairies are quietly enjoying the beauty of nature. It would not be fair, on the other hand, to lead you to believe that their quality of joy is not there; it is part of their being. They feel a loss of life and life forms, but they delight in the many forms of trees and plant life which are still there, and they give the same kind of enthusiasm to their work as before.

Though there are fewer of them, the fairies exist for the same purposes and work as they always have. And though the cities have thinned their numbers, many small city gardens actually have fairy life helping them to grow.

The pollution of the cities is not just the pollution of the urban air, which is so noticeable even to us. A more insidious kind of pollution is the proliferation of buildings, factories, schools, houses, and apartments which have taken up the land where many fairies formerly lived. Like the bird and wildlife population, the fairies have been squeezed out, and though there are still some in parks and forest preserve areas, they are not so numerous. They feel that we have encroached upon their areas more and more, leaving them less and less. There has been much use of chemical insecticides and fertilizers, both of which have a detrimental effect on the fairies' work. It is much better to use natural substances with which they can also work to inhibit damaging insects; a balance of nature between life forms (birds, insects, and lizards) is better still to control garden creatures. Chemical fertilizers, particularly the synthesized ones, are not readily workable for the fairies, whereas natural substances they understand much better, particularly such things as rotted matter which forms compost, which is part of a natural life cycle.

So much chemical and synthetic pollution is now occurring through streams and lakes that even that is causing upset for many woods and garden fairies. It is not unusual for the entire water table in an area to become polluted with such substances. These then go into the soil and again insidiously interfere with the natural cycles and harmony. Fairies are very sensitive to these things which we so casually and mistakenly do.

But even if the whole of nature is undergoing changes, the angels and fairies know there is an underlying unity in the universe. They are part of an organic whole, and this they accept. We are also becoming aware of this holistic approach to life, as greater understanding and more conscious cooperation arise with the increase in meditation and outdoor living. A link is being forged between this other, dynamic world of the fairies and us. This will become a pattern of the future.

⅍ ROSTER ⊸⅋
OF FAIRIES

AIR FAIRIES are of three general types. First are those sylphlike beings who inhabit the clouds and work with them. These are the sculptors of the fairy world. Next are the air fairies who are associated with the wind and storms. These air fairies are generally some four or five feet high, very shapely and beautiful. And last are the immense air spirits who live at very high altitudes, who resemble great dragons with huge heads, long bodies, and long tails. They are centers of energy and power of some sort. All three of these types are described in Chapter 11.

ANGELS OR DEVAS are radiant beings with great intelligence who help to guide nature by their understanding of the Divine Plan. They direct the energies of nature and oversee the lesser fairies under their care, such as tree spirits and those who might be in charge of wind or clouds.

EARTH FAIRIES consist of four main types, two of which live on the surface of the earth and two underground. On the surface, these fairies

177

range from the physically embodied tree spirits to the small common garden or woods fairies. Rock fairies, or gnomes, are one of the underground types. More specific information is given in Chapter 5.

ELEMENTALS are, as their name indicates, spirits of the elements. These creatures are evolved in the four kingdoms of elements—air, earth, fire, and water—according to Kabbalists. They are called gnomes (of the earth), sylphs (of the air), salamanders (of fire), and undines (of the water). H. P. Blavatsky, in *The Theosophical Glossary*, explains that all the lower invisible beings generated on the fifth, sixth, and seventh planes of our terrestrial atmosphere are called "elementals" and include fairies, peris, devas, djins, sylvans, satyrs, fauns, elves, leprechauns, dwarfs, trolls, kobolds, brownies, nixies and pixies, goblins, moss people, manikins, and others who belong to this classification.

FAIRIES are of four major divisions—air, earth, fire, and water. Fairies range in size from the tiny butterfly-size, to twelve-inch and two-foot ones, up to the great sylphs and tree spirits.

FIRE FAIRIES are also called salamanders.

GARDEN FAIRIES are a common kind of earth fairy.

Roster of Fairies

Gnomes are another kind of earth fairy who inhabit rocks.

Nature Spirits are those creatures of the devic kingdom who care for the different categories in nature such as the air and wind, the growing plants, the landscape features, the water, and fire.

Rock Fairies are sometimes called gnomes. Such fairies are to be found both above and below ground. The great rock fairies of the Grand Canyon are mentioned in Chapter 10 and elsewhere in the book.

Salamanders are also known as fire fairies. Chapter 10 has information on one class of these who inhabit the underground volcanic regions as well as those involved in lightning and fires above ground.

Sylphs are a form of air fairy. They are large in size, though not as evolved as those other great beings, devas. Cloud sylphs are described in Chapter 11 and also mentioned in the chapter on the hurricane, Chapter 12.

Tree Spirits, treated in Chapter 7, are larger than woods fairies and have a more physical body.

Undines (a classical or Kabbalistic name) are also called water spirits or water fairies.

Roster of Fairies

WATER BABIES are small, happy creatures who are found near the seashore and in the surf. They are a type of water fairy, but different from both those who live farther out in the deep ocean and those who dwell near streams, lakes, or ponds.